Ms. Hoyer,

Thank you for everything.
You are my favorite
person to talk about
books with. I'm gonna
miss you so much!

XO, Lulu

HOOD
FEMINISM

HOOD FEMINISM

Notes from the Women
That a Movement
Forgot

MIKKI KENDALL

VIKING

VIKING
An imprint of Penguin Random House LLC
penguinrandomhouse.com

LIBRARY OF CONGRESS CATALOGING-IN-PUBLICATION DATA

Names: Kendall, Mikki, author.
Title: Hood feminism : notes from the women that a movement
forgot / Mikki Kendall.
Description: New York : Viking, [2020] | Includes bibliographical references.
Identifiers: LCCN 2019033697 (print) | LCCN 2019033698 (ebook) |
ISBN 9780525560548 (hardcover) | ISBN 9780525560555 (ebook)
Subjects: LCSH: African American women—Social conditions. |
Women—United States—Social conditions. | Feminism—United States. |
United States—Race relations.
Classification: LCC E185.86 .K46 2020 (print) | LCC E185.86 (ebook) |
DDC 305.420973—dc23
LC record available at https://lccn.loc.gov/2019033697
LC ebook record available at https://lccn.loc.gov/2019033698

Printed in the United States of America
19 20

DESIGNED BY MEIGHAN CAVANAUGH

For the hood that gave me the tools.

Drexside, the South Side . . . forever.

CONTENTS

INTRODUCTION

My grandmother would not have described herself as a feminist. Born in 1924, after white women won the right to vote, but raised in the height of Jim Crow America, she did not think of white women as allies or sisters. She held firmly to her belief in certain gender roles, and had no patience for debates over whether women should work when that conversation arose after World War II. She always worked, like her foremothers before her, and when my grandfather wanted her to stop working outside their home, and let him be the primary breadwinner, well, that seemed like the most logical thing in the world to her. Because she was tired, and working at home to care for their children was no different to her from working outside the home. To her mind, all women had to work. It was just a question of how much, and where you were doing it. Besides, like a lot of women of that era, she had her own creative and sometimes less than legal ways of making money from home, and she utilized them all as the need arose.

She mandated education for her four daughters, who gave her six grandchildren between them, and for any number of cousins, friends, and neighborhood children around, the mandate was the same. Her answer to almost everything was "Go to school." It never occurred to any of us that dropping out was an option, because not only was her wrath to be feared, her wisdom was always respected. High school was mandatory, some college strongly encouraged, and your gender didn't matter a bit. As with work, education was something she believed everyone needed to have, and she didn't much care how you got it, or how far you went, as long as you could take care of you.

My grandmother remains—despite her futile efforts to make me more ladylike—one of the most feminist women I've ever had the pleasure of knowing, and yet she would never have carried that label. Because so much of what feminists had to say of her time was laden with racist and classist assumptions about women like her, she focused on what she could control and was openly disdainful of a lot of feminist rhetoric. But she lived her feminism, and her priorities were in line with womanist views on individual and community health.

She taught me that being able to survive, to take care of myself and those I loved, was arguably more important than being concerned with respectability. Feminism as defined by the priorities of white women hinged on the availability of cheap labor in the home from women of color. Going into a white woman's kitchen did nothing to help other women. Those jobs had always been available, always paid poorly, always been dangerous. Freedom was not to be found in doing the same labor with a thin veneer of access to opportunities that would most likely never come. A better deal for white women could not be, would not be, the road to freedom for Black women.

She taught me to be critical of any ideology that claimed to know best if those espousing it didn't listen to me about what I wanted, much less needed. She taught me distrust. What progressives who ignore history don't understand is that just like racism is taught, so is distrust. Especially in households like mine, where parents and grandparents who had lived through Jim Crow, COINTELPRO, Reaganomics, and the "war on drugs" talked to their children early and often about how to stay out of trouble. When the cops harassed you, but didn't bother to actually protect and serve when violence broke out between neighbors, lectures from outsiders on what was wrong with our culture and community weren't what was needed. What we needed was the economic and racial privilege we lacked to be put to work to protect us. Being skeptical of those who promise they care but do nothing to help those who are marginalized is a life skill that can serve you well when your identity makes you a target. There's no magic shield in being middle class that can completely insulate you from the consequences of being in a body that's already been criminalized for existing.

There's probably some value in being seen as a good girl. In being someone who values fitting in and embracing the status quo. There are rewards, however minor, for those who value being seen as that middle-class model of respectable with no inconvenient rough edges. I've never found my way there, so I won't pretend to be able to detail the value, or to judge those who can fit into that mold. I've just accepted that I never will, that I'll probably never even want to cut away the parts of me that protrude in the wrong directions. I like not living up to the expectations of people who don't like me. I enjoy knowing that my choices won't be acceptable to everyone. My feminism doesn't center on those who are comfortable with the status quo because ultimately that road can never lead to equity for girls like me.

When I was a kid I thought there must be some way I could perform being good, perform being ladylike to the point of being safe from sexism, racism, and other violence. After all, my grandmother was so determined to make it stick, it had to mean something. What I discovered was that it offered me absolutely no protection, that people took it as a sign of weakness, and that if I wanted to do more than survive, I had to be able to fight back. Good girls were dainty and quiet and never got their clothes dirty, while bad girls yelled, fought, and could make someone regret hurting them even if they couldn't always stop it. Trying to be good was boring, frustrating, and at times actively hurtful to my own well-being.

Learning to defend myself, to be willing to take the risks of being a bad girl, was a process with a steep learning curve. But like with so many other things, I learned how to stand up even when other people were certain I should be content to sit down. Being good at being bad has been scary, fun, rewarding, and ultimately probably the only path that I was ever meant to walk. I learned that being a problem child meant I could be an adult who went her own way and got things done, because I am not so focused on pleasing other people at my own expense. My grandmother was wise for her time, but not necessarily the best judge of what I needed to do. She embraced middle-class ideas of being ladylike because for her that was a path to relative safety. For me, it just left me unprepared, and I had to learn on the fly from my community how to navigate the world outside the bubble she tried to create for me. I am not ashamed of where I came from; the hood taught me that feminism isn't just academic theory. It isn't a matter of saying the right words at the right time. Feminism is the work that you do, and the people you do it for who matter more than anything else.

Critiques of mainstream feminism tend to get more attention when they come from outside, but the reality is that the internal conflicts are how feminism grows and becomes more effective. One of the biggest issues with mainstream feminist writing has been the way the idea of what constitutes a feminist issue is framed. We rarely talk about basic needs as a feminist issue. Food insecurity and access to quality education, safe neighborhoods, a living wage, and medical care are all feminist issues. Instead of a framework that focuses on helping women get basic needs met, all too often the focus is not on survival but on increasing privilege. For a movement that is meant to represent all women, it often centers on those who already have most of their needs met.

As with most, if not all, marginalized women who function as feminist actors in their community even when they don't use the terminology, my feminism is rooted in an awareness of how race and gender and class all affect my ability to be educated, receive medical care, gain and keep employment, as well as how those things can sway authority figures in their treatment of me.

Whether it's a memory of the white summer camp teacher who refused to believe that my vocabulary allowed me to know words like *sentient* or the microaggressions that I experience in my day-to-day life, I know that being a Black girl from the South Side of Chicago makes people assume certain things about me. The same is true of anyone who exists outside an artificial "norm" of middle class, white, straight, slim, able-bodied, etc. We all have to engage with the world as it is, not as we might wish it to be, and that makes the idealized feminism that focuses on the concerns of those with the most the province of the privileged.

This experience does not mean that I think of myself or anyone else as being so strong that human feelings need not apply. I am a strong person; I am a flawed person. What I am not is superhuman. Nor am I a Strong Black Woman™. No one can live up to the standards set by racist stereotypes like this that position Black women as so strong they don't need help, protection, care, or concern. Such stereotypes leave little to no room for real Black women with real problems. In fact, even the most "positive" tropes about women of color are harmful precisely because they dehumanize us and erase the damage that can be done to us by those who might mean well, but whose actions show that they don't actually respect us or our right to self-determine what happens on our behalf.

I'm a feminist. Mostly. I'm an asshole. Mostly. I say these things because they are true, and in doing so, the fact that I am not nice is often brought up. And it's true: I'm not really a nice person. I am (at times) a kind person. But nice? Nope. Not unless I'm dealing with people I love, the elderly, or small children.

What's the difference? I am always willing to help someone in need, whether I know them or not. But niceness is more than helping; it is stopping to listen, to connect, to be gentle with your words. I reserve nice for people who are nice to me or for those who I know need it because of their circumstances.

There are people in feminist circles who are nice, who are diplomatic, with soothing ways and the warm personality that enables them to put up with other people's shit without complaining. They have their lane, and for the most part I think they handle things well. But my lane is different. I'm the feminist people call when being sweet isn't enough, when saying things kindly, repeatedly, is not working. I'm the feminist who walks into a meeting and says, "Hey, you're fucking up and here's how," and nice feminists feign shock at my harsh words. They soothe hurt feelings, tell people they understand exactly why my words upset them, and then when the inevitable question of "She hurt our feelings, but she has a point—how do we fix things so that we don't harm a coworker, community, the company again?" comes up, the same nice feminist voices say the same things they had been trying and failing to convince people of before.

Only now people can hear them, because my yelling made folks pull their heads out of the sand. After the pearl-clutching about my meanness passes, what's left is the realization that they have wronged someone, that they have not been as good, as helpful, as generous as they needed to think they were all along. That's the point of this book. It's not going to be a comfortable read, but it is going to be an opportunity to learn for those who are willing to do the hard work. It's not meant to be easy to read, nor is it a statement that major issues facing marginalized communities cannot be fixed—but no problem like racism, misogynoir, or homophobia ever went away because everyone ignored it. I don't and won't pretend to have all the answers. What I do have is a deep desire to move the conversation about solidarity and the feminist movement in a direction that recognizes that an intersectional approach to feminism is key to improving relationships between communities of women, so that some measure of true solidarity can happen. Erasure is not equality, least of all in a movement that draws much of its strength from the claim that it represents over half of the world's population.

I learned feminism outside the academy first. You could almost see the ivory tower from my porch, but while reaching it was supposed to be a goal, there was minimal interaction from the students and staff at the University of Chicago with the residents of my neighborhood, Hyde Park. For all practical purposes, between the university warning students away from engaging with the neighborhood and the lack of information about how someone could even begin to access the opportunities that the university offered to people who weren't us, the ivory tower might as well have been the moon. Getting a job as a caregiver, as a custodian, or in a dining facility was relatively transparent, but as for accessing anything else? There was no clear path. The feminism at the University of Chicago on offer to the low-income Black women living in the neighborhood might as well have been a scene from *The Help*. The idea that we might have greater aspirations than to serve the needs of those born into a higher socioeconomic level didn't seem to be more than a fleeting thought for most; for a very few who were committed to a sense of equity, access came with the price of respectability. It was like getting the proverbial Golden Ticket of Willy Wonka fame, only the odds were probably better at the Chocolate Factory.

Hyde Park has gone through a lot of changes, for the better in terms of services as the population grows, and financially for the worse as gentrification means the housing prices are going up and pushing out the very people who need those services the most. Resources for residents are pouring in as many long-term residents are being forced out. Currently, the university is slightly more welcoming to locals, but is still primarily interested in being accessible to those who are (or aspire to be) middle class or wealthy. I don't know how the new Hyde Park will engage with the locals who remain the working poor, but so far all signs point to heavier policing and a complete lack of interest in maintaining the area as mixed race and mixed income.

These days, although Postcollege Me is welcome and has, in fact, spoken several times at the University of Chicago, I doubt that the girl I was would be able to even see the ivory tower, because gentrification would have forced me so far away from this beautiful area. It wasn't until I went to college at the University of Illinois that I really engaged with feminist texts as things that were meant to provide guidance and not simply to be part of the same literary canon as all the other books in the library that reflected a world I had not been able to access. There were some exceptions, but so many feminist texts were clearly written about girls like me, instead of *by* girls like me. By the time I reached a place to engage with feminism versus womanism—the former being paying more lip service than actual service to equality, the latter being closer but still not inclusive enough of people who were engaged in sex work, in vice, as a way to pay the bills and as a way of life—neither felt like they fit me or my goals completely. Girls like me seemed to be the object of the conversations and not full participants, because we were a problem to be solved, not people in our own right.

This book is about the health of the community as a whole, with a specific focus on supporting the most vulnerable members. It will focus largely on the experiences of the marginalized, and address the issues faced by most women, instead of the issues that only concern a few—as has been the common practice of feminists to date—because tackling those larger issues is key to equality for all women.

This book will explain how poor women struggling to put food on the table, people in inner cities fighting to keep schools open, and rural populations fighting for the most basic of choices about their bodies are feminist concerns, and should be centered in this movement. I will delve into why, even when these issues are covered, the focus is rarely on those most severely impacted. For example, when we talk about rape culture the focus is often on potential date rape of suburban teens, not the higher rates of sexual assault and abuse faced by Indigenous American and Alaskan women. Assault of sex workers, cis and trans, is completely obscured because they aren't the "right" kind of victims. Feminism in the hood is for everyone, because everyone needs it.

HOOD
FEMINISM

SOLIDARITY IS STILL
FOR WHITE WOMEN

As debates over last names, body hair, and the best way to be a CEO have taken center stage in the discourse surrounding modern feminism, it's not difficult to see why some would be questioning the legitimacy of a women's movement that serves only the narrow interests of middle- and upper-class white women. While the problems facing marginalized women have only increased in intensity, somehow food insecurity, education, and health care—beyond the most basic of reproductive needs—are rarely touted as feminist issues. It is past time to make the conversation a nuanced, inclusive, and intersectional one that reflects the concerns of all women, not just a privileged few.

In 2013, when I started #solidarityisforwhitewomen, by which I meant mainstream feminist calls for solidarity centered on not only the concerns but the comfort of white middle-class women at the expense of other women, many white feminists claimed it was divisive and called it infighting, instead of recognizing that the problem was real and could not solve itself. They argued that the way to fix feminism wasn't by airing its proverbial dirty laundry in public. Yet, since its inception, mainstream feminism has been insisting that some women have to wait longer for equality, that once one group (usually white women) achieves equality then that opens the way for all other women. But when it comes right down to it, mainstream white feminism often fails to show up for women of color. While white feminism can lean in, can prioritize the CEO level at work, it fails to show up when Black women are not being hired because of their names or fired for hairstyles. It's silent when schools discriminate against girls of color. Whether it is the centering of white women even when women of color are most likely to be at risk, or the complete erasure of issues most likely to impact those who are not white, white feminism tends to forget that a movement that claims to be for all women has to engage with the obstacles women who are not white face.

Trans women are often derided or erased, while prominent feminist voices parrot the words of conservative bigots, framing womanhood as biological and determined at birth instead of as a fluid and often arbitrary social construct. Trans women of color, who are among the most likely targets of violence, see statistics that reflect their reality co-opted to bolster the idea that all women are facing the same level of danger. Yet support from mainstream white feminists for the issues that directly impact trans women has been at best minimal, and often nonexistent. From things as basic as access to public bathrooms to job pro-

tection, there's a dearth of mainstream white feminist voic
speaking out against trans-exclusionary policies and laws.
one-size-fits-all approach to feminism is damaging, because i
alienates the very people it is supposed to serve, without ever
managing to support them. For women of color, the expectation
that we prioritize gender over race, that we treat the patriarchy
as something that gives all men the same power, leaves many of
us feeling isolated.

When the obstacles you face vary by race and class, then so
too do your priorities. After all, for women who are struggling to
keep themselves housed, fed, and clothed, it's not a question of
working hard enough. They are leaning in, but not in search of
equal pay or "having it all"; their quest for equal pay starts with
equal access to education and opportunity. They need feminism
to recognize that everything that affects women is a feminist
issue, whether it be food insecurity or access to transit, schools,
or a living wage. Does that mean that every feminist has to be at
every event, know every detail of every struggle? No.

It does, however, mean that the language surrounding whatever issues feminists choose to focus on should reflect an understanding of how the issue's impact varies for women in different
socioeconomic positions. The conversation around work, for instance, should recognize that for many people, needing to work
to survive is a fact of life. We can't let respectability politics
(that is, an attempt by marginalized groups to internally police
members so that they fall in line with the dominant culture's
norms) create an idea that only some women are worthy of respect or protection. Respectability narratives discourage us from

s

needs of sex workers, incarcerated women, or
...o has had to face hard life choices. No woman has
...able to be valuable. We can't demand that people
...er to live, then demand that they be respected only
work that doesn't challenge outdated ideas around
right to control their bodies. Too often mainstream fem-
...embraces an idea that women must follow a work path
...ribed by cisgender white men in order for their labor to
...ter. But everyone, from a person who needs care to a stay-at-
...me parent to a sex worker, matters and deserves to be re-
...pected whether they are in their home or in an office.

This tendency to assume that all women are experiencing the same struggles has led us to a place where reproductive health imagery centers on cisgender able-bodied women to the exclusion of those who are trans, intersex, or otherwise inhabiting bodies that don't fit the narrow idea that genitalia dictates gender. You can have no uterus and still be a woman, after all. Employment equality statistics project the idea that all women make seventy-seven cents to a man's dollar when the reality is that white women make that much, and women of color make less than white women. Affirmative action complaints (including those filed by white women) hinge on the idea that people of color are getting the most benefit when the reality is that white women benefit the most from affirmative action policies. The sad reality is that while white women are an oppressed group, they still wield more power than any other group of women—including the power to oppress both men and women of color.

The myth of the Strong Black Woman has made it so that

white women can tell themselves that it is okay to expect us to wait to be equal with them, because they need it more. The fact that Black women are supposedly tougher than white women means that we are built to face abuse and ignorance, and that our need for care or concern is less pressing.

In general, white women are taught to think of whiteness as default, of race as something to ignore. Their failure to appreciate the way that race and other marginalization can impact someone is often borne out in popular media. Consider the hamfisted misstep of Lena Dunham's HBO show *Girls*, which featured an all-white cast of twentysomething women and men living in Brooklyn, New York, being heralded as a show for all young women despite its complete exclusion of women of color. Or, more recently, Dunham and Amy Schumer's cringe-inducing conversation about whether Odell Beckham Jr. was in the wrong for not expressing any interest, sexual or otherwise, in Dunham while they were seated at the same table at the Met Gala.

Somehow the fact that Beckham was absorbed in his phone meant that he was passing judgment on Dunham's attractiveness, and not that his mind was simply elsewhere. Despite the fact that he never said a negative word, he was dragged into their personal narrative in part because of the unspoken assumption that he owed a white woman who wanted it his attention. Now, I don't expect Dunham or Schumer or feminists like them to listen to Black women or other WOC. It's not an innate skill for white people, and for white feminists who are used to shutting out the voices of men, it can be especially difficult to hear that they have the power to oppress a man. But that doesn't change the history of Black men being demonized or killed for expressing an interest in white women. Nor does it change the negative impact that a white woman's tears can still have not only on a Black man's career, but on his life. The fact that Dunham apologized and that she didn't mean to do harm is pretty much meaningless. The harm was done, and her casual racist assumptions still meant Beckham spent days in the news cycle for imaginary body shaming.

When white feminism ignores history, ignores that the tears of white women have the power to get Black people killed while insisting that all women are on the same side, it doesn't solve anything. Look at Carolyn Bryant, who lied about Emmett Till whistling at her in 1955. Despite knowing who had killed him, and that he was innocent of even the casual disrespect she had claimed, she carried on with the lie for another fifty years after his lynching and death. Though her family says she regretted it for the rest of her life, she still sat on the truth for decades and helped his murderers walk free. How does feminism reconcile itself to that kind of wound between groups without addressing the racism that caused it?

There's nothing feminist about having so many resources at your fingertips and choosing to be ignorant. Nothing empowering or enlightening in deciding that intent trumps impact. Especially when the consequences aren't going to be experienced by you, but will instead be experienced by someone from a marginalized community.

It's not at all helpful for some white feminists to make demands of women of color out of a one-sided idea of sisterhood and call that solidarity. Sisterhood is a mutual relationship between equals. And as anyone with sisters can tell you, it's not uncommon for sisters to fight or to hurt each other's feelings. Family (whether biological or not) is supposed to support you. But that doesn't mean no one can ever tell you that you're wrong. Or that any form of critique is an attack. And yes, sometimes the words involved are harsh. But as adults, as people who are doing hard work, you cannot expect your feelings to be the center of someone else's struggle. In fact, the most realistic approach to solidarity is one that assumes that sometimes it simply isn't your turn to be the focus of the conversation.

When feminist rhetoric is rooted in biases like racism, ableism, transmisogyny, anti-Semitism, and Islamophobia, it automatically works against marginalized women and against any concept of solidarity. It's not enough to know that other women with different experiences exist; you must also understand that they have their own feminism formed by that experience. Whether it's an argument that women who wear the hijab must be "saved" from it, or reproductive-justice arguments that paint having a disabled baby as the worst possible outcome, the reality is that feminism can be marginalizing. If a liberation movement's own representatives are engaging with each other oppressively, then what progress can the movement make without fixing that internal problem?

Feminism cannot be about pitying women who didn't have access to the right schools or the same opportunities, or making them projects to be studied, or requiring them to be more respectable in order for them to be full participants in the movement. Respectability has not saved women of color from racism; it won't save any woman from sexism or outright misogyny. Yet mainstream white feminists ignore their own harmful behavior in favor of focusing on an external enemy. However, "the enemy of my enemy is my friend" only works as clichéd shorthand; in reality the enemy of my enemy may be my enemy as well. Being caught between groups that hate you for different aspects of your identity means none of you are safe.

So how do we address that much more complex reality without getting bogged down? Well, for starters, feminists of all backgrounds have to address would-be allies about the things that we want. And when we act as allies, feminists have to be willing to listen to and respect those we want to help. When building solidarity, there is no room for savior myths. Solidarity is not for everyone—it cannot realistically include everyone—so perhaps the answer is to establish common goals and work in partnerships. As equal partners, there is room for negotiation, compromise, and sometimes even genuine friendship. Building those connections takes time, effort, and a willingness to accept that some places are not for you.

Although the hashtag #solidarityisforwhitewomen rose out of a particular problem within the online feminist community at that moment, it addresses the much larger problem of what it means to stand in solidarity as a movement meant to encompass all women when there is the distinct likelihood that some women are oppressing others. It's rhetorical shorthand for the reality that white women can oppress women of color, straight women can oppress lesbian women, cis women can oppress trans women, and so on. And those identities are not discrete; they often can and do overlap. So too do the ways in which women can help or harm each other under the guise of feminism.

There is a tendency to debate who is a "real" feminist based on political leanings, background, actions, or even the kinds of media created and consumed. It's the kind of debate that blasts Beyoncé and Nicki Minaj for their attire and stage shows not being feminist enough, while celebrating Katy Perry for being empowering—via the fetishization and appropriation of cultures and bodies of color. Real feminism (if such a thing can be defined) isn't going to be found in replicating racist, transphobic, homophobic, ableist, or classist norms. But we are all human, all flawed in our ways, and perhaps most important, none of us are immune to the environment that surrounds us. We are part of the society that we are fighting to change, and we cannot absolve ourselves of our role in it.

Liberation rhetoric cannot be lubrication for the advancement of one group of women at the expense of others. White privilege knows no gender. And while it makes no promises of a perfect life free from any hard work or strife, it does make some things easier in a society where race has always mattered. The anger now bubbling up in hashtags, blog posts, and meetings is shorthand for women of color declaring to white women, "I'm not here to clean up your mess, carry your spear, hold your hand, or cheer you on while I suffer in silence. I'm not here to raise your children, assuage your guilt, build your platforms, or fight your battles. I'm here for my community because no one else will stand up for us but us."

And if white women's response to that is, as it has been, more whining about how we're not making activism easier for them? We don't care. We're not going to care. We can't afford to, because while Patricia Arquette was being lauded for a speech on equal pay that she delivered at the 2015 Academy Awards, one that called for "all the gay people and people of color that we've all fought for" to "fight for us now," untold numbers of women of color were and are still fighting to get paid at all. That demand for solidarity, beyond being utterly tone-deaf, was more of the same one-way expectation.

It's not silencing, or bullying, or toxic to refuse to make anyone else's comfort more important than our lives or the lives of our children. We're not here to be Mammy or whatever other convenient archetypes movies like *The Help* often reinforce. We're not supporting characters in feminism, and we can't afford to wait for equality to trickle down to us eventually. We can't afford to believe that helping white women achieve parity with white men means that someday white, mainstream feminist ideals will reflect our needs. A hundred-plus years of history and day-to-day life teach marginalized women every day that making it easier for white women to become CEOs isn't the same as making life easier for all women.

Cultural norms that center on the advancement of the individual at the expense of the community make that kind of feminism impossible to accept as a model. For many marginalized women, the men in our communities are partners in our struggles against racism even if some of them are a source of problems with sexism and misogyny. We cannot and will not abandon our sons, brothers, fathers, husbands, or friends, because for us they don't represent an enemy. We have our issues with the patriarchy, but then so do they, as the most powerful faces of it aren't men of color.

My husband may not always understand how misogyny impacts me, but he can absolutely grasp what it means when a boss's or a coworker's racism is an impediment. We sit together at that table, even if we don't face the exact same battles in every aspect of life. Women in communities of color must balance fighting external problematic voices with educating those inside our communities who are bad actors, and we expect feminism to do the same work on itself.

Intersectionality isn't a convenient buzzword that can be co-opted into erasing Professor Kimberlé Williams Crenshaw, who coined the term to describe the way race and gender impact Black women in the justice system. An intersectional approach to feminism requires understanding that too often mainstream feminism ignores that Black women and other women of color are the proverbial canaries in the coal mine of hate.

It's not always easy to confront a problem when it occurs, but ignoring it is dangerous. Take Hugo Schwyzer, the man whose predatory and abusive behavior sparked the conversation about what solidarity in feminism means. When Schwyzer admitted on Twitter that he had spent years alternating between abusing students and spouses and targeting women of color, the response from feminist outlets that had published him was to distance themselves. Many white, mainstream feminists claimed not to have known what he was doing; one of the reasons that argument didn't hold up was the years of blog posts, emails, and articles written by him for their publications where he gleefully detailed his history. It was a redemption narrative that required no actual change or even accountability for prior behavior. Not only was the emperor naked, so was everyone else in his court. What happens to us first will eventually happen to white women, so enabling abusers like Schwyzer can only lead in one direction, yet unchecked racism often renders women who should be allies as complicit in the abuse until they are targets too.

Fast-forward slightly to Gamergate, a loosely connected campaign of misogyny, racism, and harassment. Zoë Quinn was the first target, but the men who went after her, who churned up the rage and stoked the hate, practiced their craft on Black women first. Because Black women are seen as having no selves to defend, it was us standing with each other while mainstream, white feminism looked the other way. By the time the threats were aimed at big-name white feminists like Sady Doyle, Jessica Valenti, and Amanda Marcotte, the question shouldn't have been "How did this happen?" It should have been "Why didn't we do more to stop it sooner?"

Many white feminist pundits were shocked in 2016 when Trump was elected, and it became clear that despite his abominable record on women's issues, race, class, gender, and education, the majority of white women voters (some 53 percent) voted for a man who promised to mistreat them. One who made jokes about grabbing their pussies because he was certain his fame would sway them into accepting his atrocious behavior. Trump wasn't offering a bright, shiny future with equality for

all. In fact, most of his campaign promises centered on the idea that the real problem was immigration. He promised a future with lower competition levels, where white women who live in fear of a mythical Black or Muslim man could feel that their fears were justified, that their racism was justified. Instead of appealing to women on the basis of equality, he appealed on the basis of fear, and for many white feminists, they were shocked to discover that the solidarity they had never offered wasn't available to them either.

The shock that 53 percent of white women voted for Trump was sadly hilarious. It turned out that even among white women, solidarity was only for some of them. For women of color, especially Black women, it wasn't a surprise. It was the same racism we had always seen masked as feminism playing out in real time. Feminism that could ignore police brutality killing women of color, that could ignore the steady disenfranchisement and abuse in local and national politics of some women based on race and religion, wasn't about equality or equity for all women; it was about benefiting white women at the expense of all others. There was a sense that when the targets of oppression weren't white, it was fine to vote based on "economic distress" and not solidarity with other women. Only it turned out that the policies that followed have so far served to increase that distress, disadvantaging everyone who isn't a rich white male.

When I first met the writer Gail Simone, I made her gluten-free triple-chocolate cupcakes as a gift. While we were talking that day, she asked if I was interested in writing comics. The comics industry is a white, male-dominated space, and Gail

could have treated the niche she has carved out for herself as something to defend from other women. Instead when I said yes, she went out of her way to help me get into the industry. I've since learned that she does this pretty often. She knows she has power and privilege and she uses it to help others whenever she can. Sometimes being a good ally is about opening the door for someone instead of insisting that your voice is the only one that matters.

Gail's a great writer and editor. She pushed back against a misogynistic trope of killing women in comics to further the stories of male heroes. She started out as a hairdresser and probably fails to meet someone's definition of *respectable* every day. She's doing the work, though, and changing the way an industry functions for women and with women, one book at a time. Sometimes solidarity is just that simple. Step up, reach back, and keep pushing forward.

GUN VIOLENCE

My grandfather saved my life when I was six. He grabbed my hair and yanked me out of the middle of a gunfight between two strangers as I was walking out of a beauty shop. I remember that my bangs got a sizzling little trim from a round, and I was more focused on that (I really wanted short bangs for reasons that now escape me) than on the fact that a few more inches and my hairstyle wouldn't have mattered. I am not afraid of guns. Actually, I love guns. More accurately, I love shooting them. I go to the range to shoot weapons I would never want on the street; I talk online occasionally about my time in the military—a time when I had access to many types of weapons, from guns to grenades. Periodically, I even mention my grandfather and his guns. To me, guns are tools; the people wielding them are the deciding factor in whether that tool is used safely or unsafely. That doesn't mean I think you should take guns to brunch, or to the grocery store, or to a movie theater.

What does feminism have to do with guns? After all, guns aren't a feminist issue, right? Except they are. They just might not be a feminist issue for your life. Not right now, anyway. But many women, especially those from lower-income communities, face gun violence every day. The presence of a gun in a domestic violence situation makes it five times more likely that a woman will be killed. Women get killed by these guns because they are available, because their partners are violent, because an accident with a gun is more likely to be fatal, because of a dozen mundane reasons made worse by the availability of weapons. Although we tend to focus on the impact on young men who are exposed to gun violence, girls are likewise gravely affected. Girls drop out of school at nearly the same rate as boys in an effort to avoid having to pass through places where shootings are common—that is, in an effort to *survive*. Mothers bury their children because of gun violence. Families are irrevocably changed by guns. Mainstream feminism has to engage with gun violence as an everyday occurrence in the lives of some women. It can't be treated as a distant problem when in some neighborhoods, bullets are as common as rain. In order to adequately address the needs of the girls and women who deal with the consequences of what amounts to a full-scale public health crisis every day, mainstream feminism has to be listening, advocating, and providing resources. A twelve-year-old girl was shot on her porch a few blocks from my house while I was writing this chapter. The gun used to injure her didn't belong on the street. She's one of hundreds of girls who will be impacted by gun violence this year, one of almost two hundred thousand children impacted by gun violence since the Columbine shootings in 1999. You may think that gun violence is a distant problem, nothing to do with you, but if you pause, if you look around, if you look outside the bubble that privilege has created where you don't have to worry about gun violence on a regular basis, you'll see it's a public epidemic that we ignore. Every state, every city, and every income level has been impacted by gun violence.

It's tempting to pathologize gun violence as a problem that only exists in the hood, in places where ostensibly there is no promise of a future and supposedly no one is innocent, so everyone deserves whatever happens to them. The media often presents a narrative of gun violence as the consequence of Blackness and poverty intersecting, and thus the key to avoiding it is to stay away from poor Black neighborhoods—what we have seen with white flight or de facto sundown towns. We have been led to believe that conditions are so bleak in the inner city that there's nothing left to protect or support. But while white people measure their safety in cubic feet from Black people, the reality is that while Black people in the hood are more likely to be victims of gun violence, it can and does happen everywhere. And increasingly so. From Las Vegas to Parkland to Orlando, mass shootings are a near daily occurrence in America. Every time, Chicago gets trotted out as proof that gun control won't work, but the reality is that Chicago's problem with gun violence is America's problem with gun violence.

It's true that in any area socially and economically isolated from the mainstream, crime rates are higher, and that poverty often leads to illegal markets. But from bootlegging to the drug trade, violence is most likely to proliferate where there is no other recourse for solving disputes. And that is why we see increasing rates of gun violence in rural areas, as well as higher death rates, even as gun violence declines in urban areas—though it's not a fact commonly cited in the news.

What compounds the problem of violence in the hood is the long history of isolated Black communities in America not being able to trust law enforcement as, over time, they have proven themselves to be largely indifferent to violence against marginalized people. The same attitudes from law enforcement can be found in rural areas, where help may be farther away and weapons are a key part of life because hunting for food is still common. In both cases, gun culture often develops out of necessity. While the number of people in law enforcement in rural areas may be lower, which suggests an illusion of greater safety because of lower populations, class and racial divides reflect the wider societal biases. Crime rates have been dropping for decades all over the country, but higher population numbers in urban centers mean more crime because there are more people and more media coverage. Meanwhile, in rural areas, it's not that crime rates are substantially lower; they are just less likely to be covered in the same way by whatever press may exist in the area, if there's any local media at all.

White flight suburbs and former sundown towns are a prime example of places where the crimes that are happening aren't highlighted because the criminals in question are white. In the absence of racial diversity, class can take center stage. Even though white privilege doesn't disappear when poverty comes into play, the reality is that poverty limits access to the power and sense of safety that come with being one of the property owners who our current policing system is designed to protect. Though our culture frames the white working class as important, as a primary concern, the reality is that although poor white people fare better than poor Black people, ultimately in situations without an Other (read: someone not white), class differences make poor white people the target of oppressive structures.

The idea that poor white people are morally and socially inept, too ignorant to be a part of the wider world, excuses them from the racist systems that they lack the access to create even when they benefit from them. It's that internal oppression that whiteness enacts on itself that helps create a narrative that the world is out to get working-class white people—and that people of color are specifically at fault for their problems. Add in the ways racism positions guns as the solution to crime, and these conditions breed a gun culture that embraces violence while resisting any efforts to curtail access to weapons, regardless of who gets hurt. America's history has been defined by its violence, the question of how to respond to it largely answered by law enforcement obtaining bigger and better weapons to counter the ones held by criminals. We've taken war weapons to the streets and homes of civilians with no idea what harm these weapons can do, or that escalation is never a solution.

We know that education is key to success in America and around the world. But almost three million children per year are exposed to gun violence once you factor in violence from crime, in homes, accidents, and suicide. Gun-related deaths are now the second-leading cause of death for American children, who are fourteen times more likely to be killed with guns before age fifteen than children in other high-income countries. Americans aged fifteen to twenty-four are twenty-three times more likely to die from gun violence. Sixty percent of American children and teens who are victims of homicide are killed with guns. That averages out to sixteen hundred gun deaths per year. For children under the age of thirteen facing family violence, the presence of a gun at home ups their risk of being killed, so much so that two-thirds of child fatalities from domestic violence are caused by guns.

Not surprisingly, Black children and teens are most at risk: they are four times more likely than white children and teens to be killed with guns. When home isn't safe, school isn't safe, and the streets aren't safe, then what kid can focus on school to the exclusion of the danger? It's a rare few. Girls face a double problem of being at risk and being ignored in most efforts to combat gun violence.

We can't pretend that the education of girls abroad is important and ignore how many girls are undereducated or uneducated in America as a result of gun violence. The bullets that didn't hit me still changed me. Though it has gotten better over time, when I was first diagnosed with PTSD, I thought all my behaviors were normal. I've often reacted to apparently innocuous things in ways that can seem jarring to those who grow up without the threat of gun violence. Hypervigilance and anxiety are part of how you stay alive in communities where gun violence is a constant, and it took a long time for me to recognize that these traits were my response to trauma.

To this day, I can tell you about all the times a gun was in my face, and I've never been in a gang, never been involved in criminal activity. And while getting my hair cut by a bullet makes for a good story, it's unremarkable when we consider the statistical likelihood of gun encounters in America. Likewise, the time a guy tried to rob my mother at an ATM and pointed a gun at me to make her comply is as American and mundane as apple pie. The girls who get woken up by gunfire, who learn that a car doing a slow creep is a reason to get down, who die because they were standing near a crowd where a gunman opened fire all have stories that matter, and they deserve our attention, even as we lose sight of them under the avalanche of coverage that prioritizes everyone but them.

If gun violence is an issue for all of us, what makes it specifically a feminist issue?

We focus anti–gun violence programs on everyone but the girls and women at risk. Too often, we frame them as the ones who bear witness to the consequences, and not the ones who face them. But we know that gun violence touches girls at all points of life. In 2016, the Violence Policy Center documented that Black women experience the highest rates of gun homicide out of any group of women, and much of that can be attributed to instances of intimate partner violence. "Compared to a black male, a black female is far more likely to be killed by her spouse, an intimate acquaintance, or a family member than by a stranger." And unfortunately, this is something that I can speak to personally.

I have been in more than one abusive relationship. The first of them was when I was in high school. I didn't know it at the time, would not have called it abusive—he never hit me. He never had to hit me, because at that time I was so busy trying to be "good" that I mistook being a doormat for being a lady. High school is shoddy relationship central, so eventually I broke up with the guy who made me feel like crap, who cheated on me constantly, and called myself too strong to ever put up with anything worse than that. I was one of those girls who always knew that I would leave if a man ever hit me. Because that's what you do, right? You walk away and never look back. That works very well in theory, but in practice, it's often just a nice lie to tell yourself. Comforting, even. I tell this story because sometimes the story of your life is the story of a lot of lives.

I had a habit of falling for people who weren't nice to anyone except me. I didn't notice that about myself, didn't think about what it meant that I would accept the attention of someone callous and cruel as long as they were charming to me. In retrospect, my high school boyfriend treated me like an emotional yo-yo, ready to promise forever one minute and breaking up with me the next in a cycle that had shorter and shorter honeymoon periods. When things were good, I thought we were perfect. When things between us were bad, he was verbally abusive, and prone to being physically intimidating if not outright threatening. Though I would not have admitted it then, I tied myself in knots to appease him until I finally got myself off the proverbial string by ending the relationship on my terms for once.

A partner who's only nice to you when it suits them doesn't need to be loved into being a good one, I thought. They need to be dumped so you can move on with your life. Lesson learned, right? Right. Except I didn't learn the most important one, the one about partners you have to appease to feel safe. Not then, anyway. When I met my first husband five years and a handful of boyfriends later, and he was super attentive and interested, I had no problem ignoring his flaws. Even the ones that were giant red flags, like the fact that he was married to a woman who had been his high school sweetheart, and who, he assured me, he was ostensibly divorcing after only a year of marriage. I was so busy wrangling my own flaws, and I loved him so much, I assumed that we could make anything work. I never asked the right questions, and I resisted listening to my own instincts about people who have not left their last relationship before they start a new one. I was very good at lying to myself. Great at lying to other people too.

Anyone who pointed out that the man I loved might not be such a great guy was quickly assured he was, that he'd gotten married young and just made a mistake. When his divorce was finalized, I felt vindicated instead of played, even though it had taken a year after he first told me that they were divorcing for their marriage to be legally over. Despite the fact that he was only divorced a literal five minutes when he asked, I was thrilled to be engaged. Not only did I say yes to getting married, I moved right into a full-time, committed relationship with someone who hadn't let the ink dry on the divorce paperwork, much less resolved any issues that might have led to that relationship ending.

We got engaged, married, and moved into base housing as the military allowed it. And the red flags I had ignored turned into emotional land mines almost immediately. I was far from the flawless victim. He yelled, I yelled; and the first time he hit me, I hit him back. It wasn't until I had locked myself in a room and listened to him kick the door down while I crouched on the floor that I started to think I was maybe in over my head. Probably. And even then I didn't call it quits. I didn't even call the military police; a neighbor did. And the first MP to arrive on the scene called it "mutual assault"—that is, until his supervisor arrived and, looking at all 120 pounds of me and all two hundred pounds of my husband, replied, "You mean self-defense?" Because he could see that eighty pounds and six inches wasn't a fair fight in any universe.

We didn't split up. We went to counseling and apologized and rationalized. It was stress and poor communication, we reasoned. He was charming when it suited him, and I am a hard person to live with, and so on. I thought loving someone meant trying to make it work. Especially with a baby on the way who deserved an intact family. We made it through other incidents, tried counseling and some measure of separation, and moving to new places, and all the things you do when a relationship that shouldn't have happened dies by inches.

We had a child, we moved apartments and even countries, and we kept trying to be a family despite the violence that seemed to be the other child we were raising. We went back to civilian life, and for a brief moment I lied to myself again and blamed the military, and not the fact that we were locked in a toxic dance that couldn't get better. The last time that man hit me was during a fight that started over something mundane, but I changed the locks and called the cops myself that time. "It wasn't any different from what happened before," is what I might have told you then. We had a fight, and I wish I could tell you that I knew for certain we were done. We were certainly close to done, our relationship a flawed pressure cooker always riding the line of exploding.

But a year into knowing it needed to be over, weeks into what should have been a slow and amicable dissolution, the proverbial steam whistled so loud it was too far and too much to ignore. In the moment, as mad as I was, somehow I was still shocked when he pinned me to the fridge with one hand around my throat, aimed his fist just so to knock me out, and released. Then he dragged me across the floor, took my keys, and left. Our two-year-old son saw all of it, and I will forever regret not getting out earlier; but I also know that my tenuous plans to get out hinged on getting into a place I could afford on my own, getting childcare, and crafting a life where no matter what he did or didn't do, I could make it.

I wasn't quite there, but when that last bout of violence erupted, I knew the clock on my perfect plan had run out. I had a place I could mostly afford with only my name on the lease, and I got on with it. That didn't mean the violence was over exactly; it just moved out of my house. He still sent me angry, abusive emails and text messages, he stalked and harassed me, and he still threatened violence despite restraining orders and arrests. But the good news, the best news? He didn't have a gun. He could threaten, he could yell, he could hit me, but what he couldn't lay his hands on was a projectile weapon that would have turned survivable rage into that split second that can't be taken back. I got lucky, because we were in Illinois, a state that enforces the restriction on gun ownership for anyone with a recent history of domestic violence. Was he angry enough to kill me if a gun had been available? Yes. He might argue something different now, but I know what I saw in his face, and I know how hard he punched me, and that a hard head meant I ended up with bruises and ringing in my ears and not something worse.

Intimate partner violence isn't the only risk of violence that Black women face. Police violence, particularly being collateral deaths in police misconduct, is a risk that is rarely discussed in feminist circles but is something that Black Lives Matter and campaigns like #SayHerName attempt to address. Their work is made more difficult not only by the lack of any official data but also by community norms that center on cisgender men.

I could be any of the women we have seen brutalized or killed by police in recent years as videos proliferate. I could have been that little girl down the street who was shot in the ankle while I wrote the draft of this chapter, or I could be Rekia Boyd, a young Black woman in Chicago who happened to be standing next to a man holding a phone to his ear when an off-duty police officer, mistaking the phone for a gun, opened fire and shot her in the head. The man with the phone was shot in the hand. Rekia died at the scene. She committed no crime, and the officer who shot her served not a single day in jail despite admitting he shot over his shoulder as he drove away. He wasn't working, he was a newcomer to the area who owned property nearby, and still the gun in his hand took a young woman's life.

I can't tell you how many times I have been in contact with police officers over the years. I've just been lucky about the kind of officer I have encountered. I have been verbally abused by a police officer, threatened, harassed, but never assaulted. That's not a statement about who I am or how I engage; it's just the luck of the draw. There's a tendency to assume that the women who do have negative interactions are at fault, but if you can be shot standing still or asleep in your own home, can be brutalized for seeking help, then it would seem that engaging the police at all is inherently risky.

I live in a city where we sit on a porch or in the park on warm nights. Should socializing with my neighbors include the risk of death? Some of the best moments of my life have included hanging out in the park with friends. Just shooting the shit, you know? Have we been loud? Probably. But there's a reason it was an off-duty cop new to the neighborhood and not a patrol car that encountered Rekia Boyd. People who grow up in the area wouldn't call the cops over something as mundane as people hanging out in the park. Because they know that any encounter with Chicago police can escalate quickly, and no one wants that on their conscience over some hollering. I don't believe that a large group of Black bodies equals crime, but I know a lot of people trumpeting on and on about the joys of gentrification who do.

So, there are new neighbors who talk about how great the properties are and how scary the longtime residents are even if they never quite say why they find them so frightening. The cop mistaking a phone at someone's ear for a gun? That's part of the same system of "scary Black man" myths that killed Trayvon Martin in Florida. It's so embedded in America's collective psyche that we're criminals that it probably didn't even occur to the cop who killed Rekia in Chicago to consider that Black people could be out enjoying one of the warmest March days in history, and that their presence shouldn't be a reason to suspect anything more than an impromptu block party. No weapons were recovered at the scene, a woman is dead, and a man is injured and has been charged with assault for standing outside talking on his phone. That's what it means to be Black in America. That's what it means to be a Black woman in America. When annoying a new neighbor carries the risk of being shot, the question isn't whether gun violence is a feminist issue; the question is why mainstream feminism isn't doing more to address the problem.

In order to build that bright feminist future, we need to invest in becoming the kind of society where resolutions to disputes, safety concerns, and crimes aren't reliant on someone's access to a weapon. That means shifting our cultural assumptions about what constitutes safety, as well as changing our public and private policies to minimize the overreliance on violence as a solution. We need to be willing to accept that a legacy of bigotry means that moving to a new place requires you to understand that everyone has a right to be there, to have their culture and community. We need to be willing to listen to victims of intimate partner violence, to take their fears seriously the first moment they report feeling uncomfortable or unsafe, instead of invalidating or second-guessing them because we think someone looks harmless. As a culture, as feminists, as potential and actual victims, we're often too socially and emotionally entangled with dangerous people to recognize the risk until it is too late. We need to support violence-intervention programs at all levels, and not assume that gun violence is a systemic issue in the inner city and episodic everywhere else.

We also need to stop normalizing hate and stop assuming hate speech is harmless, regardless of who it targets or who says it. While it is true that not everyone who makes bigoted comments will go on to commit violent acts, our normalization of that kind of hideous rhetoric serves as tacit permission for the people with those views to escalate to violence. Intervening early can save lives. It's not about bubbles (liberal or otherwise); it is about treating gun violence as a community health problem and devoting resources to curing it.

It's time to treat domestic violence and hate speech as the neon red flags that they are and take the necessary steps to reduce the risks instead of hoping that they'll go away. It's time to treat gun violence like a feminist issue—not just when it plays out in domestic violence or mass shooting but also when it impacts marginalized communities. We will either work to make it possible for all of us to be safe from gun violence or none of us will be.

HUNGER

My first marriage ended in divorce, and afterward, I was on food stamps, I had a state-funded medical card that gave me and my son access to medical care, and I was living in public housing. I was fortunate at the time that this particular set of social safety nets allowed me to leave my abusive ex and stay gone. I could raise my child in relative comfort and safety. Today, many of those safety nets have been greatly diminished, and in the case of public housing, it has nearly fallen away completely in many areas. We know in the abstract that poverty is a feminist issue. Indeed, we think of it as a feminist issue *for other countries*, and that we are in a place where bootstraps and grit can be enough to get anyone who wants it bad enough out of poverty. But the reality is that it takes a lot more than gumption. I was lucky: I'm educated. My grammar school and high school curricula prepared me for a college education. I joined the army to pay for my degree, and since I was in Illinois, a state that has a tuition-free Veteran Grant Program for state schools, it didn't matter that I was doing this in the days before the GI Bill paid enough to be useful.

I was poor, and it wasn't easy, but I had the handholds it can take to be upwardly mobile when you're marginalized and life is working against you in other ways. A childcare subsidy meant that when my ex didn't pay child support, my child was still able to attend the high-quality preschool on my college campus. I got a bachelor's degree in four years, went on to work full-time, and took a host of other perfectly boring but necessary steps that brought me to where I am today, with an advanced education, a wonderful family, and a career that I enjoy. If this were the usual heartwarming, feel-good tale about single parenting and poverty, you might come away thinking, "Well if she could do it, why can't everyone else?" And you might expect me to say, "It was hard, but I learned so much, and I remember that time fondly."

What I remember is hunger. And crying when I couldn't afford a Christmas tree. I remember being afraid that I couldn't make it. That I would lose my child because I couldn't provide. It's hard to take a rich woman's children; it is remarkably easy to take a poor woman's, though. As a society, we tend to treat hunger as a moral failing, as a sign that someone is lacking in a fundamental way. We remember to combat hunger around the holidays, but we judge the mothers who have to rely on food banks, free or reduced lunches at school, or food stamps for not being able to stand against a problem that baffles governments around the world. Indeed, we treat poverty itself like a crime, like the women experiencing it are making bad choices for themselves and their children on purpose. We ignore that they don't have a good choice available, that they're making decisions in the space where the handholds are tenuous or nonexistent.

The women in these circumstances may not have a grocer that sells fresh produce, or at least not one that sells produce they can afford. They may be working too many hours to be able to prepare food, or they might be dealing with food storage issues. The story behind that pack of chips and soda at a bus stop is often far more complicated than any ideas of a lack of nutritional knowledge, laziness, or even neglect. Sometimes the food you can access comes from gas stations, liquor stores, and fast food restaurants and not a fully stocked grocery store, much less a kitchen.

We know that food deserts exist, areas where groceries are scarce and what is available may be unfit for human consumption. But food insecurity is more complicated than simply the ability to access food. There's the question of what food costs versus what people can afford. If you live near a grocery store but you can't afford to shop there, then it doesn't matter that you're not in a food desert. You're still hungry. And hunger doesn't have an age limit; there are food-insecure children, food-insecure college students, and food-insecure elders. Some forty-two million Americans are struggling with hunger. Statistically at least half of that number are women, but given gender bias in wages, the real percentage is something like 66 percent of American households struggling with hunger are headed by single mothers.

Women and children account for over 70 percent of the nation's poor. Unfortunately, existing safety net programs have failed to take into account the reality of poor women's lives. The money a household makes for many state and federal programs, like Temporary Assistance for Needy Families (TANF), as well as childcare subsidies, leaves a wide gap between what is needed and what is available. Take Illinois, for example, where a single parent receiving TANF for one child is eligible for a maximum of $412 a month. Even the most ardent proponent of mandating independence should realize that that isn't enough money to cover the basic needs of two people. As a culture, we don't have sufficient provisions for helping women and families escape poverty. In fact, we often create artificial and unnecessary barriers, like limiting unemployment insurance to full-time workers, which leaves part-time workers with no assistance if they lose their jobs. We rely on charities to address acute hardships like hunger before the food stamps come in, and to respond to the homelessness crisis when HUD has a waiting list that can span decades in some areas.

We know that without a home, individual families suffer and fall further into poverty. Yet eviction rates and the price of food continue to rise all while wages remain stagnant, and the cycle gets even harder to navigate. Especially when work requirements are introduced, ones which ignore that childcare is a necessity for women with very young children. Is it possible to work a full-time job when you can't even afford part-time childcare? Or is this a policy guaranteed to create even higher hurdles? Paid maternity leave is a wonderful cause, but what happens after the baby is born and you weren't making enough money to support one person, much less navigate these new, higher expenses?

Alleviating women's poverty is a critical feminist issue. Yet when we talk about hunger and food insecurity, we rarely talk about it in these terms. Why? Because in many mainstream feminist circles, the people talking about these issues don't know what it is to be food-insecure in the long term. Things like food stamp challenges, where someone lives on a budget similar to that of someone living on food stamps for a week or a month, make good stunts, but they don't influence public policy. If anything, people who engage in those stunts are more likely to pat themselves on the back for making it through and perhaps donate to their local food bank, and then forget that the problem exists.

Hunger has a lifelong impact, shaping not only someone's relationship with food but also their health and the health of their community. Hunger, *real* hunger, provokes desperation and leads to choices that might otherwise be unfathomable. Survival instincts drive us all, but perhaps none so strongly as that gnawing emptiness of hunger. Whether we call it being hangry or something else, hunger is painful even in the short term. And yet we rarely speak of it as something for feminism to combat, much less as something that is uniquely devastating for women.

Consider the way that we handle programs like SNAP or WIC in America. We place myriad restrictions at the federal and state levels on how those funds can be used. As a society, we then try to rationalize the limits by pointing to cases of fraud, which, aside from constituting less than 1 percent of all public welfare cases, are usually the kinds of things that can best be explained by the ways you have to manipulate your life to get through poverty. It's easy to say no one should ever sell food stamps, harder to justify that stance when you remember that people need things like pots and pans to prepare their food. They need working refrigerators, stoves, and storage solutions to keep out the vermin so commonly found in the subpar housing that is often the only option for those living at or below the poverty line. Food stamps don't even cover basic household cleaning and hygiene products, much less things like diapers and menstrual pads.

You can be very comfortable asserting that poor people don't know anything about nutrition if you ignore the fact that perishable fresh foods require not just the space to store and prepare them, but the time. Boycotts of terrible retailers are a wonderful idea until you realize that they are the only option in some areas. The question that the would-be protester should then ask themselves is, who is being hurt more? The corporation, or the people who rely on it for access to food? These are questions without easy answers, to be sure. But that's life in the hood. That's being poor not just in America, but around the world.

Mainstream feminism pays excellent lip service to the idea that poor women are supported, but in practice, it often fails to interrogate what constitutes support. Hood feminism as a concept is not only about the ways we challenge these narratives, it is about recognizing that the solutions to many problems—in this case hunger—can be messy and sometimes even illegal. Poverty can mean turning to everything from sex work to selling drugs in order to survive, because you can't "lean in" when you can't earn a legal living wage and you still need to feed yourself and those who depend on you. When mainstream feminism fails to consider these options as viable, when it relies on the same old tropes rooted in respectability, it ignores that for many, a choice between starvation and crime isn't a choice. Feminism has to be aware enough, flexible enough to encompass the solutions that arise in a crisis. When feminists fail to recognize the impact of hunger, they can unwittingly contribute to the harm done by failing to offer the slightest bit of compassion or grace to those who are facing only bad choices. But hunger is devastating, its impact painful in the short term and horrifying if it endures over time or across generations. If we're going to say that this is a movement that cares for all women, it has to be one that not only listens to all women but advocates for their basic needs to be met. You can't be a feminist who ignores hunger. Especially not when you have the power and the connections to make it an issue for politicians in a meaningful way. Fight against hunger as hard as you fight for abortion rights or equal pay. Understand that this isn't a problem that can be addressed later.

As income inequality increases and the wealth gap widens across racial lines, there is no question that for some women, for some communities, hunger is going to move past bad nutrition into outright malnutrition. If we don't make combating hunger a priority now, it will make itself a priority when far too many women and their families are suffering from it.

WHY IS IT that we're more inclined to create programs to combat obesity than ones that meaningfully address hunger? Proponents of things like a soda tax hold their plans up proudly, but never talk about why soda is such a staple in homes where food insecurity is a problem. They don't talk about the fact that soda is shelf stable, is cheaper than juice, and it tastes good. They don't consider the fact that low-income consumers don't have to worry about it going bad, about it containing mold like Capri Sun products did before their most recent packaging changes, or fungicides like some orange juice brands did before the FDA increased testing. And they would never acknowledge that consumers don't have to worry about soda manufacturers facing the same risk of lead-tainted water like residents in Flint, Chicago, and so many other cities, because those companies can and do buy the filtration systems needed for clean water in creating their products in any setting.

Instead, proponents of policies like soda taxes insist it is about health, and they point to dubious claims that obesity is a disease that can be cured by taxing soda. Messages declaring "Soda is so bad for children" play out with images of kids going to a soda machine and receiving diabetes instead of a ginger ale. If sugar was a toxic chemical guaranteed to bring about illness in all who consumed it, then these images might make sense. But the hyperbolic assertions that obesity can be cured by taxing soda ignore studies published by the Centers for Disease Control and Prevention that prove that numbers on a scale have very little to do with health outcomes.

Politicians use fatphobia and make obesity a scapegoat to deflect attention away from the policies that have adversely affected the health of low-income communities. Fitness is a much better measure of health, and one that requires a multipronged approach that's much more labor intensive than a tax. It includes children having access not just to recess at school, but to safe neighborhoods where playing outside doesn't put them at a greater risk of violence. It requires them to have access to food on a regular basis. Research shows that things like exercise, fresh produce, clean water, clean air, and access to health care are all major factors in good health. Midnight basketball and other after-school, weekend, and summer programs didn't just reduce violence by giving at-risk youth an outlet, they also created patterns of healthy behavior. They made it easier for families to be active and to feel comfortable sending their kids to play outside without fear. These programs and others like them provided food, nutrition classes, and more without judgment—and they have largely been shuttered.

In the end, soda taxes have very little to do with health. It's an easy platform for politicians and their backers, but if the concern were really public health, the focus wouldn't be on regressive taxes as a solution. Nor would the counties that adopt such taxes be using revenue from it to fund everything but measures that would bring healthy, affordable food options into low-income communities. What's more, if the aim is to lower overall sugar consumption, it hardly makes sense to target only one form of it. A can of regular soda has 39 grams of sugar, but a cup of cocoa has 49 grams of sugar. Frappuccinos? Some can have as much as 102 grams of sugar. Those other options are socially acceptable, and the dairy is a source of protein and vitamins, but the amount of sugar consumed is significantly more. Socially acceptable sugar isn't healthier simply because it costs more than a can of Pepsi. It's clear that the concern here is less about the healthfulness of sugar and more about finding another revenue source for cash-strapped municipalities.

Soda taxes hit the people with the fewest options the hardest, because in a food desert, too often the "healthy" options are also the most expensive. Low-income parents already struggling with food insecurity and neighborhood violence are now being told that their children's health problems (symbolized by weight) are their fault for having only hard choices available. Which option is healthiest when your choices are tap water with lead in it, bottled water that already carries an additional tax, overpriced juice, milk being sold past the sell-by date, and soda? What problems are solved by putting one more tax burden on the backs of those least able to afford it? Policies that serve as "food police" tend to raise stigma rather than help families and individuals who need better access to food.

And this isn't just a problem in the inner city. Indeed, grocery prices on a reservation or the lack of options in many rural areas with only one or two stores are a testament to how difficult it is to keep food on the table. Hunger is a problem in every country and in every county for those who lack the resources to feed themselves or their families.

A WOMAN STOPPED ME one day years after I was done with hunger as something to manage in my personal life, and she asked for help buying groceries. I gave her what I could and went on with my day. It cost me some money that I could afford to lose, and we parted ways pretty quickly. I almost forgot about it, to be completely honest—I subscribe to my own internal version of the butterfly theory when it comes to kindness. One day, I was in the same area, and a woman I didn't recognize paid for my groceries. She wouldn't take my money and looked at me when I tried to argue and said, "*I* didn't argue with *you* now, did I?"

It hit me then that she was the same woman who had asked for my help with groceries. She had been my neighbor the whole time. And while I didn't remember her, she remembered me very well. This isn't a story about how great I am. You see, when I bought those groceries, I said something offhanded about remembering how hard it can be at the end of the month when stamps run out. I assumed she was there because she was getting inadequate help. Actually, she wasn't getting any help; she'd lost her job and her spouse, and her life was just crumbling, and I had insulted her somewhat by suggesting she was on food stamps. It hadn't been intentional, and when she mentioned it, I apologized. She laughed at me and said she'd eventually gotten over it, that being able to eat and feed her kids for those few weeks got her to get some help.

It worked out, she got back on her feet, and she was doing fine when I saw her, but she had been both grateful and angry at me for a while. It's a funny place to be, and I understand it, but I might not be able to explain it to anyone who has never experienced that loss of pride, that shame that you simply cannot do it all on your own no matter how hard you work. What she needed was the food, the cash. What she didn't need was my assumptions. Or to have to feel grateful, or that there was something to be ashamed of in seeking help. And maybe if we could admit that most women are poor, that many are struggling to feed themselves and their children or their other family members, we could start addressing this issue that affects most women with all the power it requires. We could stop acting like food insecurity is a sin or a shame for any individual and treat it rightfully like an indictment of our society.

The good news is that women in these communities are working to combat hunger with everything from community gardens to food cooperatives. Whether it is transportation for those who lack access to well-stocked stores or pooling resources à la Stone Soup to feed kids in the summer when school is out, there is no shortage of grassroots initiatives devoted to bringing food to those who need it the most.

The bad news is that none of those programs are enough to effectively combat hunger on their own. They need more. More resources, more employees, more efforts by the government to solve the problem across the country. And they don't have the connections, resources, or time to lobby politicians and provide services. Charity may begin at home, but it is fundamentally incapable of solving a societal ill without some measure of government-funded programs that are less focused on being restrictive or punitive and more focused on making sure that the most vulnerable are cared for regardless of income.

Attempts to tie access to food programs to labor, to respectability, to anything but being a human in need are ultimately less about solving the problem of hunger and more about shame. While proposed cuts to SNAP or other government food security programs are often justified by the perceived prevalence of private programs, it is incredibly unlikely that food banks or charities would be able to fill the gap should food assistance programs be reduced or dissolved in the coming years. SNAP provides approximately twelve meals to every one meal provided by charities. Programs like WIC and SNAP exist because prior administrations have understood the massive disparity between what private charities and the government can do.

We know what happens when charities can't make up the difference: the pictures of bread and soup lines in history books and the stories from our grandparents about starvation and the Great Depression are easy to mine. Despite conservative narratives about "lazy people," roughly 40 percent of SNAP recipients are already working, and simply using food stamps to supplement their salaries and keep themselves capable of being in the workplace. Many of the remaining 60 percent can't work because they are minor children, elderly, or caregivers for vulnerable family members. Even if the working poor who make up the SNAP population are able to pick up a second job, get a raise, or find another way to cut living costs to afford food, there's still the question of the effect on the children and seniors who may depend on those working relatives for caregiving.

Because issues around affording childcare, elder care, or other services bring about other difficulties for those people who are already struggling, the addition of proposed work requirements would move people into the workforce who are not prepared and can't afford to be there. And then there's the question of what jobs they will be able to access. After all, if you don't have the skills, need more education, have health issues, and so on, then losing SNAP benefits would only make your chances of staying employed nearly nonexistent. It's a no-win situation that hinges on bootstrap rhetoric instead of logic or facts. Food stamp recipients are mostly children and elderly or disabled people, in households where at least one adult is working but doesn't make enough to pay for all of the household expenses. There is a very small percentage of recipients without dependents, and among that group of able-bodied adults without dependents, most already work or are seeking work. They're cycling in and out of low-paying jobs that have a lot of turnover: seasonal employment, retail, or other industries that regularly experience lulls in demand for labor. These recipients are on SNAP on a temporary basis and rely on the program when they're unemployed or underemployed. The myth that they are somehow a burden ignores decades of job statistics that show that combating hunger is a boon to the economy.

Increasing access to food should not be a controversial topic, but apparently we live in a culture that begrudges children, elders, unemployed people, and the working poor full, nutritious meals. Even though marginalized people who need help with food security are seen as second-class citizens, they are a key part of the food economy. In rural areas, migrant workers cultivate and collect the food that ends up on the tables of the people who want to write policies that would starve them. Despite the fact that seasonal labor is the bulk of the workforce for our food supply, their access to resources is severely curtailed. And once the food reaches the market, workers in grocery stores are often underpaid and among those who have issues with food security.

Women in the workforce are a key part of the food processing and preparation that makes feeding families possible, but at every level, they are at risk of exploitation and deep discrimination. Between low wages and a higher-than-average risk of sexual harassment and assault, marginalized workers in rural and urban areas are responsible for unpaid and low-paid work only to be excluded from decision making and leadership positions around food security. The people responsible for making sure that food is safe, accessible, and palatable are some of the lowest paid.

For families headed by women and by other marginalized people, feminism has to come through to combat food insecurity, from higher prices for fresh foods to insufficient government funding for programs that address hunger on a systemic level. Without support from feminists with privilege and access, families facing food insecurity will suffer despite their best efforts. Hunger saps your energy, your will; it eats up the space that you might have used to achieve with the need to survive. As feminist issues go, there are none that span more women and their families than this one.

Food is a human right. Access to adequate food and nutrition allows communities to thrive; it allows women to fight for all their rights. Food security allows for marginalized women's participation in political and other organizational spaces, key for defending their interests against other forms of structural oppression.

Bringing about feminist changes will only be truly possible if mainstream feminism works to combat discrimination in all its forms, from gender to class and race. True equity starts with ensuring that everyone has access to the most basic of needs.

OF #FASTTAILEDGIRLS
AND FREEDOM

Like a lot of others, I was a fast-tailed girl before I really understood what those words meant. It's one of those colloquialisms you hear as a child in certain communities that is half-warning, half-pejorative. To be a "fast-tailed girl" is to be sexually precocious in some way. You are warned both not to be a fast-tailed girl, and also not to associate with "those fast-tailed girls." Sometimes it is shortened to "fast," but either way, it is presented as a bad thing. The elders who typically use it are often attempting to protect young women from being perceived as Jezebels. When I started the #FastTailedGirls tag on Twitter with my friend journalist Jamie Nesbitt Golden in December 2013, thousands of women came together in an outpouring of emotion. When you consider the long history of sexual violence perpetrated against Black women in America, the roots of this particular aspect of respectability politics are easy to grasp. Here respectability politics are not just about clothes or speech, they are about governing how young Black women engage with their own sexuality as it is developing. This is meant to be protective, but it is often oppressive.

However well meaning, warnings about avoiding being fast are a deeply flawed response to the problem of sexual violence. Why? Well, you don't actually have to be sexually precocious to be labeled a fast-tailed girl. Perception is everything, and so a host of perfectly normal, age-appropriate behaviors like talking to boys, wearing shorts, and wearing makeup, or even going through puberty early are enough to convince some people that you're headed for trouble. And once that perception is entrenched, any bad things that happen to you are automatically your fault. Like other expressions of Madonna-whore complexes, there is an idea that bad things don't happen to good girls.

Research done over the past decade by the Black Women's Blueprint and the Black Women's Health Imperative, two organizations that work to address the specific needs and concerns of Black women, show that some 40 to 60 percent of Black American girls are sexually abused before age eighteen. And those girls are likely to be labeled fast-tailed retroactively by people who need to believe that what happened to them was their fault. Because they must have done something to entice a man's interest, the victims watch their abusers evade scrutiny and ultimately justice. This is nowhere more evident than in the recent condemnation of R. Kelly, whose marriage in 1994 to a then fifteen-year-old Aaliyah, as well as alleged video evidence of him urinating on another teenager, and his subsequent trial on child pornography charges weren't enough to end his career, much less impact his freedom. In turn the girls were blamed for being near him, for not knowing better, for not being prepared to navigate interactions with an adult predator who had celebrity and wealth on his side. I can't say that I'm surprised by Kelly's ability to avoid consequences. Often it is easier for the community to focus on the girls than on potential predators.

My grandmother warned me at length about being fast and about hanging out with fast-tailed girls over the eight years that I lived with her. When I later moved in with my mother at the age of twelve, I learned that a pubescent body was enough to make me fast in the eyes of some people. I was something of a tomboy despite family efforts to turn me into a little lady, and while the lectures from my grandmother about who I should befriend remained the same, my mother wielded the term *fast* like a weapon. When a man stared at my suddenly prominent nipples on a windy day, I got in trouble for being fast. I never told my mother about the elderly family friend (truly *old*, he wasn't much younger than my grandfather) who'd started hitting on me long before our miniskirt battles, or about the babysitter who'd molested me and whose nickname for me still makes me nauseous.

What my mother saw as me being fast-tailed was really the fumbling efforts of a survivor struggling to figure out my own sexuality without someone else's input. Because everything I did was already wrong in her eyes, I was convinced I couldn't tell her what had happened to me. That she would see it as my fault, much the way she interpreted my blossoming body as an invitation to grown men. Our already strained relationship deteriorated further over the years that followed as my body and my interests developed past the boundaries of what she deemed acceptable. Clothes, friends, even phone calls were battlegrounds for a war with no winners and no hope of resolution.

As an adult I can look back and see that my mother was probably afraid for me, because I was so far from her idea of a respectable young lady. I hung out with boys, wore midriff-baring shirts and miniskirts when I could, and practiced flirting like some people breathe. I wasn't Jezebel or Lolita, but she couldn't see that, and I didn't have the words to explain that I was fighting to control my own body. For young Black American girls there is no presumption of innocence by people outside our communities, and too many inside our communities have bought into the victim-blaming ideology that respectability will save us, not acknowledging that we are so often targeted regardless of how we behave. The cycle created by racist narratives and perpetuated by the myth of the fast-tailed girl is infinitely harmful and so difficult to break, precisely because of the ugly history of sexual violence against Black women and other women of color.

I was lucky enough to be a smart girl who could write, even if I was incredibly socially awkward, and while my teachers loved me, it was the kindness of the girls we often see framed in media as the Mean Black Girls that really gave me access to a wider, healthier life. I grew up with the boys who became gang members, but it was the girls who were in their path who taught me how to differentiate between who was dangerous in general and who was dangerous to me specifically. By the time we were ten years old we needed to be able to tell the difference, because no one was coming to save us but us.

Most of us had parents or guardians, had people who did their best to shelter us, but the first steps toward independence were also steps into a broader world full of danger. There we faced more than just the patriarchal church leaders, the grandfather who expected you to be ladylike, or even the teachers who hated everything from bracelets to silliness from girls like us. We had to worry about all the other social dangers of police and predators and learn to navigate a world where poverty meant that the street sometimes spoke to us, and sometimes outright shouted invitations.

For the girls who couldn't code-switch, the ones who struggled with school and home, there was always the street. The girls who could run away often did, because they weren't safe at home, and the swaggering braggadocio of the streets sometimes made them less anxious. They had internalized the stress, had found that the danger they might face at home was too much to stick out. Media always makes wild, violent girls out of the ones who resist the mantra to "stay home, be ladylike, be silent about your fears," and it's true some of them end up violent.

But girls and young women are far more often the victims of violence than the perpetrators of it. The fact that they are often in harm's way because they have no other options is erased from discussions of what has happened to them, of what might happen to them again.

Yes, girls in that age category are sometimes complicit in those kinds of crimes, and are ultimately responsible for at least some of their choices. But that doesn't begin to accurately reflect the extent of the ways that patriarchy influences girls in under-resourced neighborhoods. Some girls end up trafficked; others become so involved in gangs that the gang takes the place of their families. The hypermasculinity of gang culture can seem like protection if you've never been safe. And the lines between types of violence get very blurry when you are exposed to it constantly. The long-term emotional impact can be severe for girls who have been exposed to violence either as victims or as witnesses. Girls in violent areas can suffer from higher rates of posttraumatic stress disorder, depression, anxiety, and substance use.

Girls of color in a patriarchal system have experienced more abuse, violence, adversity, and deprivation than protection. Yet programs that focus on "at-risk" girls tend to focus more on job skills and preventing pregnancy and not on equipping them with better coping mechanisms. We need to shift the conversation about systems from vague assertions that work is empowering and early pregnancy is bad to one where we support the healing and healthy development of girls and young women in every community.

While the suffragette and labor movements of the early twentieth century brought about great strides toward equality for white women, for Black women in particular and women of color in general, unpunished sexual violence was and remains a constant threat. Despite the narratives espoused by lynching advocates, white women were not the ones who were most at risk from sexual violence. Black women were expected to adhere to every aspect of respectability pushed on them by Jim Crow laws as well as by community norms established in the wake of slavery. However, it didn't really matter how Black women and girls dressed or behaved, because white men could and often did assault them for sport.

Unlike white women, Black women had not even the thin veneer of legal protection on their side. It wasn't until Recy Taylor, a twenty-four-year-old Black mother and sharecropper, was attacked in Abbeville, Alabama, on September 3, 1944, by six white men that the possibility of legal recourse for such crimes even entered the national discourse. The Committee for Equal Justice for Mrs. Recy Taylor was formed by Rosa Parks and several other civil rights leaders of the time to attempt to get some measure of justice for Mrs. Taylor. The crime, which garnered extensive coverage in the Black press, never saw the indictment of the accused, but it did help pave the way for women of color to be able to turn to the law for help.

FROM ROSA PARKS and the Committee for Equal Justice for Mrs. Recy Taylor to Korean feminists pushing for the Japanese government to pay reparations for victims of the wartime practice of "comfort women," women of color have always organized to combat sexual violence. More recently groups like Incite! and the Human Rights Project for Girls have highlighted the reality that sexual abuse is a key factor in young women of color ending up in the school-to-prison pipeline. When the work centers on the most marginalized targets of sexual harassment and abuse, it benefits not only their communities, but all communities.

Although there was no real justice for Recy Taylor, we can look at the Daniel Holtzclaw verdict in Oklahoma and see the impact of a history of organizing: Holtzclaw, a former police officer, was convicted of sexually assaulting twelve Black women and sentenced to 263 years in prison after organizers brought media attention to his case, and the police department actually held him accountable instead of trying to minimize or conceal his crimes. It's not enough to focus on the most visible victims; we must use every opportunity to challenge rape culture at all levels. We must challenge violence from not only those we think of as rapists but also those who administer this system that privileges rapists over their victims, and that normalizes the harassment and abuse of the most vulnerable.

In any given week you can find articles from mainstream, ostensibly feminist sites that turn rape prevention into a circle jerk of not quite victim blaming. They're filled with tips about how to fight a stranger, what not to wear or drink, and where not to go. Emily Yoffe's 2013 *Slate* piece "College Women: Stop Getting Drunk" pushed for a dry campus life for women so they could avoid being sexually assaulted. Sometimes these articles even advocate for forcing victims to testify against their will, as illustrated in Amanda Marcotte's 2014 *Slate* piece "Prosecutors Arrest Alleged Rape Victim to Make Her Cooperate in Their Case. They Made the Right Call." Though these pieces are generally well meaning, they ultimately frame rape as something that a potential victim can prevent if they learn the steps of this peculiar dance that is trying to avoid being possibly assaulted, the immediate response is often one of several questions ranging from "What were you wearing?" to "Why were you there?" to "Had you been drinking?" The answers to those questions can never be relevant—ultimately victims are assaulted because someone chose to attack them.

Instead of tips on how to not be a rapist, how to teach people not to rape, or even on creating therapeutic outlets for potential rapists, we find a half dozen tips on preventing a mythical stranger from raping an able-bodied, alert, physically fit person with excellent reflexes and an exceptional amount of luck.

These tips never address disability, differences in fight-or-flight (or freeze) adrenaline responses, or even the reality that most assailants are known to their victims. Often, the articles are dissected and derided by readers within hours of being posted. So why do they keep showing up? The easy answer is that they make people feel better. After all, if you think you can stop someone from being hurt with a bit of advice, then you can also protect yourself by following the tips. It's a tidy bit of feel-good magical thinking that absolves us all from confronting the reality of what it will take to end sexual assault. After all, no one has a quick and easy solution for any crime, much less for one like rape, that can manifest in so many ways and often leads to a victim being revictimized during the reporting process.

It's easy to blame the patriarchy, to rightfully point at the men who rape and hold them accountable. What's harder is to notice the women who sometimes passively direct rapists toward their victims by contributing to the hypersexualization of women of color under the guise of empowerment. That rape is always the fault of the rapist is true and accurate, but it is also an incomplete assessment of rape culture. Beyond the space that is cultural appropriation, or even the bizarre periodic "accidental" bouts of blackface, there's the problem of theoretically feminist white women who think "sexy Pocahontas" is an empowering look instead of a lingering fetishization of the rape of a child. The same imagery they claim to find sexually empowering is rooted in the myth of white women's purity and every other woman's sexual availability.

There's nothing empowering about the idea that the road to their sexual freedom is making a fetish costume out of a culture. And I know that some will argue that these are just harmless costumes. While there's certainly no attire that will protect you from sexual assault, the cultural framework that positioned Black women as un-rapeable exists in a different but similarly dangerous way for other women who are not white. This isn't about respectability politics, because these outfits are rooted in a mockery of the source cultures that they claim to honor. It's imagery that is directly offensive in part because it plays on racist tropes that fetishize the bodies of women of color. Things like Victoria's Secret's Sexy Little Geisha lingerie campaign, where most if not all of the models were white women. Or any number of Instagram-popular festivals like Coachella, where a nude or nearly nude white woman will post pictures in a fake war bonnet with provocative captions mirroring everything from Chanel's cowboy-and-Indian-themed fashion show to ads for cologne. Defenders of the imagery will often argue that they mean to honor the nations they think they are imitating and that they are doing no real harm. But the rape statistics for Indigenous women don't match that argument.

One in three Indigenous women will be victims of sexual assault, and the abuser is most likely to be a white man. Moreover, white men are not only most likely to assault women from this group, they are also the demographic most likely to sexually assault white women. Statistically speaking, white men are most likely of all groups of men to commit sexual assault. But too often it is framed as though the attention of white men isn't dangerous for women who live outside that narrow range of protection white supremacist rhetoric affords some white women.

Objectification isn't harmless, and the ways it can play out span race, class, gender, and sexual orientation. When fetishization goes beyond consensual kink and into a green light to target communities, then we have to break down how sexual empowerment narratives can be twisted to feed into the problem.

When the humanity of women of color is erased by these dehumanizing tropes, the duty of feminists who claim to fight rape culture is to push back. Instead, all too often women of color are left to explain and fight on their own, because some of the same feminists who understand objectification and fetishization when it impacts them suddenly can't understand their role in the problem. And while the reasons for this vary, they can largely be attributed to the notion that the women donning the costumes feel "powerful, sexy, and exotic," as though their feelings matter more than the lives of those they are giving rape culture tacit permission to harm.

When we talk about rape culture, we have to think about who is at risk. Indeed, who is being put at risk by the ways that racist tropes are bolstered in feminist circles? We know that racism plays a role in every walk of life (well, we should know that), and that includes not only who is believed when they report being assaulted, but how much they have to fear reporting an assault.

Yet we know that resources like culturally competent counselors, safer spaces like shelters, even police officers who are equipped to take a report without doing further harm are lacking for sex workers, trans women, and many women of color— and still we see attempts to insist that reporting it will stop sexual assault. But if the people most likely to commit assault are also the ones most likely to be insulated from consequences, then what good are we really doing for victims?

We know that colonialism and imperialism rely heavily on the use of rape as a tool of genocide. That dynamic of racism and misogyny intertwined continues to haunt our culture even as we attempt to combat it. We know that women of color are more likely to be victims of police brutality and less likely to be supported, much less protected. When we encourage victims to turn to the police, but ignore that the second most common form of police misconduct is sexual assault, how are we helping victims feel safer?

While we don't know how many police officers actually engage in sexual assault as part of police brutality, we do know from a report published by CNN in October 2018 that between 2005 and 2013, police officers were charged with at least four hundred sexual assaults. Additionally, during that same time span, officers were accused of over six hundred incidents of groping. What's missing from these statistics is whether the officers were on duty; whether the numbers include domestic cases between officers and their own partners; and what percentage of all encounters are being represented. And we don't have that information precisely because police departments do not make it available. It goes without saying, however, that these aren't the kinds of numbers that can make a victim feel safe going to the authorities even before you get into the sad reality that reporting rarely leads to justice.

Rape is a violent act, but it is one of the final steps in the violence against marginalized people that is embedded in the fabric of human society. Like in any abusive relationship, the violence starts with manipulation, coercion, and propaganda. Rape has been used to repress, to undermine, and to control because power functions in the same awful ways in every generation. The fear of mythical Black rapists that was used after the Civil War to justify the white mobs that terrorized the Black communities has been subsumed into a broader anti-immigrant narrative under the current administration. Popular media continues to perpetuate racial stereotypes that were part and parcel of imperialist propaganda, particularly about women of color. Portraying Black women and Latinas as promiscuous, American Indian and Asian women as submissive, and all women of color as inferior legitimizes their sexual abuse. Portraying men of color as sexually voracious and preying on innocent white women reinforces a cultural obsession with Black-on-white stranger rape, at the expense of the vastly more common intra-racial acquaintance rape.

Justice is not served by racism, no matter how hard it is peddled by politicians and white supremacist narratives as a way to protect women. Not replicating these harmful narratives is part and parcel of ending sexual violence against women. It would be easy to claim the fallacy that "no true feminist thinks that way" as a means to absolve the broader movement of responsibility. But the historical devaluation of some women's rights to sexual and reproductive autonomy has shaped the way we think about what it means to have the freedom to be safe from sexual violence.

Columbus reveled in his ability to assault Indigenous women with impunity, and that attitude permeates our culture to this day. The fact that enslaved Black women did not have the right to refuse the sexual demands of white men created the idea that Black women were un-rapeable, because, after all, they had no virtue to protect. Over and over, white women are held up by white supremacy as the only virtuous women, but then the tightrope narrows. How you're dressed, whether you were drinking, how developed your body is, and more become factors in justifying sexual violence. Ignoring the treatment of the most marginalized women doesn't set a standard that can protect any women. Instead it sets up arbitrary respectability-centered goalposts against which all women are supposed to measure their behavior. That's not freedom; that's just a more elaborate series of cages that will never be comfortable or safe. Any system that makes basic human rights contingent on a narrow standard of behavior pits potential victims against each other and only benefits those who would prey on them.

Rape culture, a system that positions some bodies as deserving to be attacked, hinges on ignoring the mistreatment of marginalized women, whether they are in the inner city, on a reservation, are migrant workers, or are incarcerated. Because their bodies are seen as available and often disposable, sexual violence is tacitly normalized even as people decry its impact on those with more privilege. Rape culture doesn't happen in a vacuum; it is built consciously and unconsciously by societal norms. It requires everyone else to buy into respectability as safety, then immediately position every step away from that standard as culpability for being violated. Rape culture is normalized and ratified not only by patriarchal notions of ownership and disposability but also by attempts to combat it by buying into the framing that the patriarchy creates. Respectability politics, victim blaming, and fetishization can only create a fundamentally flawed and dangerous response.

To quote Gwendolyn Brooks, "We are each other's harvest; we are each other's business; we are each other's magnitude and bond." But if we believe that only some people deserve safety, that the right to your own body has to be earned through adhering to arbitrary rules, then are we really seeing each other as equals? As human beings at all?

Obviously, the problem isn't going to be resolved by a hashtag like #FastTailedGirls, or by a few thought pieces, but the first step to finding a solution is admitting that there is something to be fixed. We'll need to keep having these conversations, keep being open to the idea of working against these socially ingrained notions so that we can stop them. The problem is not unique to Black communities, to the cisgendered, to heterosexuals, but as with every other community it touches, the internal work must be done so that the external problems can be addressed. This is a sickness that touches so many, and we need to work as partners with each other to heal it. Yet this is not a call for outside assistance; this is a message for those outside our communities to address the racialized misogyny in their communities that perpetuates the idea of Black women as Jezebels. Any solution to this problem will require society to address all the racist, sexist tropes that frame women of color as sexually available and un-rapeable.

Freedom has a price that we all must pay together. It's not going to happen if the stats used to combat rape culture are based on the harm done to marginalized women, but the beneficiaries of any advances are only those who have some measure of protection via white privilege. We know that trans women of color are especially vulnerable to violence; we know that whole communities of Indigenous women have nowhere to turn for safety. We know that danger comes from the very people who are supposed to be our protectors, whether that be the police or men in our communities. Rape culture is pandemic and must be fought unanimously or we will never defeat it.

We must look at the fact that even in emergency situations, white bystanders are less likely to help Black people than each other. We have to ask ourselves why the study "White Female Bystanders' Responses to a Black Woman at Risk for Incapacitated Sexual Assault" shows that even young white women in college are less likely to help potential victims of assault if they are Black. We have to ask why white undergrads said to researchers that they would be less likely to help Black women because they felt less personal responsibility for them. Or why they perceived Black victims as experiencing more pleasure in situations that they recognized as dangerous for white women.

Although white women are aware that they are also at risk because their privilege doesn't protect them from sexual violence, a combination of racism and sexism lends itself to a significant number of them ignoring the consequences of their actions for other communities. Whether it is contributing to hypersexualized narratives around women of color, ignoring the dangers faced by those communities, or undermining those who come forward, they sometimes flex what power they do have in ways that are oppressive while they continue to imagine themselves as victims with no power to oppress.

When you can't count on solidarity for women in danger, when bystander intervention isn't a solution because white female bystanders may feel that a Black woman's plight doesn't deserve their attention because race has a more powerful effect than gender, then we aren't really battling rape culture. And the battle will continue to evade us until we fight the internalized -*isms* inherent in the movement.

When Lena Dunham felt the need to dispute the claims of actress Aurora Perrineau, a victim of sexual assault who happened to be Black, because the accused was her friend, it had everything to do with race, whether Dunham admits it or not. Perrineau had accused Murray Miller, an executive producer on Dunham's *Girls* show, of having sexually assaulted her, and Dunham flew to the man's defense, citing "insider knowledge" that rendered the claim false. A year later, Dunham was issuing an apology, one that tap-danced around the ease with which she seemed to offer support to everyone who was the "right" kind of victim, or more accurately, the "white" kind of victim, until she was challenged repeatedly. Most of the apology centers on herself, and even the part that specifically addresses Aurora Perrineau centers on Dunham and her own journey.

> *To Aurora: You have been on my mind and in my heart every day this year. I love you. I will always love you. I will always work to right that wrong. In that way, you have made me a better woman and a better feminist. You shouldn't have been given that job in addition to your other burdens, but here we are, and here I am asking: How do we move forward? Not just you and I but all of us, living in the gray space between admission and vindication.*
>
> *It's painful to realize that, while I thought I was self-aware, I had actually internalized the dominant male agenda that asks us to defend it no matter what, protect it no matter what, baby it no matter what. Something in me still feels compelled to do that job: to please, to tidy up, to shopkeep. My job now is to excavate that part of myself and to create a new cavern inside me where a candle stays lit, always safely lit, and illuminates the wall behind it where these words are written: I see you, Aurora. I hear you, Aurora. I believe you, Aurora.*

Public acts of racism appear bolder and more numerous in the Trump era, but it's important to remember not only that they're not new but also that the real harm is often done in private. When we ask why victims don't report assault, why conviction rates are so low, and whose fault it is that rape culture persists, the answers are disheartening and interconnected. "They won't get justice," "We don't care about protecting victims or punishing their attackers," and "Everyone's," because ultimately it is all down to the insidious ways that rape culture is built and sustained in some of the same places, from homes to schools to churches, where it does the most harm.

And though I have largely focused on the objectifying narratives around the bodies of women of color and how mainstream feminism fails to engage them, I am in no way saying that sexual violence is only a concern of cis women. While cis women experience some of the highest rates of sexual assault, trans and gender-nonconforming people also face a heightened risk. And from a college campus to the military to a prison, no place is safe. Mingled among the victim-blaming tropes that position location as a factor for victimization is the reality that rapists attack in any environment where they think they can succeed.

And attempts to place bans on women in the military and trans women in bathrooms, or to assert that people who have been imprisoned deserve to be subjected to sexual violence, is just feeding into rape culture from different angles. Assertions that sex workers can't be assaulted or that they exist as a release valve to prevent sexual violence are fundamentally rooted in narratives that render bodies disposable without interrogating how deep into rape culture these so-called feminist narratives have fallen.

We must remember that every victim of sexual violence does not deserve it, did not invite it, and is not responsible for the culture that would blame the victim instead of the perpetrators. We must understand that not only do we have a responsibility to not blame victims, but that we must actively work against cultural memes that render it acceptable to foster the hyper-sexualization of potential targets based on skin color, gender expression, or age.

I'm not raising any young girls, but I do have plenty of them in my life. As part of my commitment to changing the way that we talk about young women's sexuality, rape culture, and gender, I've gone out of my way to teach my sons about consent. To talk to them about respect as well as the basic decency of not being a harasser. It's a tiny step, certainly not a solution to the problem. But it is a place where I can begin to intervene on a personal level. More important, as a whole, feminism has to focus on change inside individual communities as well as across the world. We have to shift the focus on anti-rape narratives away from what victims can do to prevent it and toward teaching people not to be predators in the first place. We have to stop ignoring the cultural messages we are complicit in transmitting that say some people deserve to be sexually assaulted.

Feminism must challenge these narratives, or risk yet another generation being told that respectability can save them while they watch admitted harassers and assailants face no consequences for their crimes. The problem has never been the ways that victims don't tell, so much as it has been that some victims aren't seen as valuable enough to protect.

IT'S RAINING PATRIARCHY

I grew up with a traditional grandfather, and after my mother started dating the man who would become my stepfather when I was five, I became the daughter of an equally traditional man. They're the kind of men who opened doors and pulled out chairs and sometimes put their whole foot sideways down their throat when it came to gender. My grandfather wasn't a bad man, but he was every bit of what you might expect from someone born in 1919. He was at best benevolently sexist, and at worst sometimes outright misogynistic—though I didn't have that language for his behavior when he was still alive. I can look back, though, at the things he said about what women could or should do, the ways he balked at me being a tomboy, and see that he bought into the strict gender roles of his time, and then he had to deal with massive social changes over the course of his seventy years, as well as his daughters and granddaughters rejecting so much of what he expected from us. My dad is a little better. By the time he met my mom, I was already showing the tomboy inclinations that were the subject of a lot of family arguments. Sometimes he opens his mouth and the patriarchy comes tumbling out on any topic ranging from what input he thinks my husband should have on my choices for my body to what I do for a living. Then he pulls back (possibly because of my reactions) and says something about "modern women." Most days my dad just buckles up, shakes his head, and lets my complete lack of investment in the traditional narratives he holds dear wash over him.

He loves me, though he doesn't understand me, but then I don't completely understand him either. For instance, I am not totally sure I understand his attachment to being so patriarchal that he once asked me how my husband felt about my hysterectomy. I told him something brisk about it being my body and my husband not getting a vote, and we left it at that. He understands and appreciates that I am educated and employed, but he just can't quite wrap his mind around why my husband and I are so averse to traditional gender roles in some key (to him) ways. His attitude is patriarchy in action, which from anyone else would be an unequivocal source of conflict with me, but navigating patriarchal norms is complicated when it comes to the men who raised me and the man I love.

I can comfortably talk about feminism and the hood and so many things about masculinity and its damaging impact, and yet the most I could do with my dad was set a quick, crisp boundary. To be fair, we've never discussed the hysterectomy again, and he doesn't say things like that about my body to me anymore, but the fact is, he holds positions that I don't believe in. The same is true for many women in communities like mine, where the sexism comes from people we love and who we respect, even when we disagree with them.

Feminists need a more realistic understanding of the complex nature of patriarchal influences on marginalized communities. Whether we are talking about inner cities or rural areas, the semi-segregated nature of most working-class communities plays a huge role in the way patriarchal narratives are embraced. These communities are largely socially and culturally homogeneous, and a great majority of the residents are hyper-concerned with respectability because of white patriarchal messaging about respect being reserved for those who are law-abiding, religious, and at least somewhat socially conservative.

The majority of residents advocate conservative values and aspire to a better life for their children. Younger residents tend to share their parent's or guardian's values: they work hard, they avoid getting enmeshed in any crime or violence around them, and they tend to either avoid drugs entirely or consume far fewer than their white working- and middle-class counterparts. Yet they face a disproportionate risk of arrest and incarceration for even the most mundane of misdemeanors.

In all communities, there is a minority group of youth that rebel against at least some of their community's values. They may engage in some measure of illicit activity. Some have been pushed out of school and are chronically out of work, while others are voluntary dropouts or at least not pursuing any further education beyond high school. They lack the skills and the credentials for higher-paying jobs, and cannot subsist on low-wage jobs without some way of supplementing their income. They skirt the poverty line, but generally stay above it through underground economies.

Because of a lack of respect elsewhere, the men in these scenarios value a measure of subservience and submission from women that is intended to make up for what they can't receive in the wider world. Customs that seem to directly contradict feminism, like making a man's plate and serving it to him, are part of a configuration of norms, values, and habits that are, at their core, mainstream inside the community. Outside these communities, the idea of a woman being expected to prepare and serve her significant other can be seen as an indication that she is not his equal. As with any custom, there are certainly ways that it can be regarded as harmful, but it's one of many practices specific not only to a community but also to a relationship. My husband is more likely to plate up my dinner because he cooks more than I do, but I'm more likely to make the plates for the kids. That's what works for us. And even though the practice is heavily debated inside our community, as a wordless expression of affection and respect, it can be incredibly validating. Making a man's plate and other similar practices exist in large part because the only place a Black man might experience respect is from someone in his family. Even now, in 2019, the outside world often fails to respect Black people, much less Black men.

It's also here that the hypermasculinity that can seem so aggressive plays out as an assertion and defense of respect. A lot of narratives about what it means to be a man, to be someone who stands up and stands out in a community as a leader, are created in this space where respect is not only earned, but must be constantly demanded. Whether that means raising your voice or resorting to violence, carving out a space for yourself in a world that denies your right to exist is important. Gang culture, the bravado that permeates and creates toxic masculinity, is also a twisted method of self-defense from the broader world. While the desire for name brands can seem counter to what is needed in low-income communities, there's a defiance of respectability politics playing out in the attachment to everything from gym shoes to hoodies. Suits, ties, and demure dresses didn't protect our ancestors from violence before or during the civil rights movement, and they won't protect residents of the inner city now, no matter how often people try to blame victims of racism for how they are dressed. Individualism, materialism, and a reverence for "traditional" gender roles is filtered through a lens of intracultural norms.

Counter to that centering of hypermasculinity is Black feminism, which recognizes that fighting the white supremacist patriarchy outside the community is different than fighting the toxic masculinity inside the community. There's a desire to see the same men who are so adversely impacted by racism succeed, but not at the expense of Black women. That means a careful balancing act of prioritizing the safety and health of all without ignoring the harm the patriarchy has done or could do.

Though such culture can be incredibly toxic, particularly where the demand for respect is enforced by the use of emotional and physical violence, in many ways it is simply the inverted image of iconic values, a push for equality, if not equity, as seen through a fun-house mirror. It's toxic masculinity as medicine for a disease wrought in oppression. When you are used to seeing a broader social narrative that positions some people as disposable, the instinct is to replicate it inside smaller communities, and because it has been so normalized, it is difficult to imagine a different social order. While communities of color are certainly affected by the white patriarchal narratives presented as desirable culture through the media, much of our internal patriarchal dynamic in communities of color is homegrown, an outgrowth of the cultural responses that originated more in reaction to the institutionalized violence of colonialism and imperialism. It's not the Donna Reed fantasy of the 1950s, that pallid ode to Jim Crow–era myths about the role of moderately well-off white women who were figuring out how to balance work and home with spouses who earned enough for them to afford a housekeeper.

The toxic elements of Black and Brown cultures of hyper-masculinity are born in part out of the impact of low wages, where the option of a woman not needing to supplement the household income was never on the table. Where the only response available to overly aggressive law enforcement was protest, but protest rooted in an expectation of potentially lethal consequences. This is a culture where women were largely in charge not because they had fought to be, but because the men in their lives and communities were being imprisoned or killed with little rhyme or reason. The consequences of white supremacy inside communities of color has been exceptionally harsh, especially since the war on drugs began. Mass incarceration has damaged so many communities, removing many of the more traditional social customs around family from the realm of possibility. For the men who were left, being respected often centered on what was happening inside their homes because there was no chance of it outside.

Too often the role of crime in low-income communities is rendered as laziness or a refusal to take care of a family, or otherwise situated in narratives that ignore how much of masculine identity centers on being a provider and a protector. It's difficult to do either when you can't get a job, and yet the pitfalls of resorting to vice are increasingly obvious. If you're absent from your family and community for years because of incarceration, then when you do return, you are unlikely to have the skills needed for any kind of healthy progressive relationship. You are even less likely to be able to get a job that lets you support yourself, much less a family.

In many ways, the patriarchal standards that formed in the aftermath of the war on drugs are different from the ones our grandparents and parents experienced. With the removal of so many from the community to serve jail sentences that spanned decades instead of months, families had to restructure themselves. New standards developed that were less about traditional nuclear families living in isolation and more about intergenerational and interdependent living. Everyone needed to work as inflation rates rose and Black wealth did not.

New standards ratified the idea that Black women working was the norm, but with so many men incarcerated, heterosexual women in particular often felt they had to compete for partners by tightly adhering to the most patriarchal of standards—standards they felt were of utmost importance to the men—to offer to work, take care of all household duties, to be submissive . . . the list is more than any two women could reasonably be expected to do. Yet the "pick me" culture, a phenomenon where some women announce their willingness to adhere to these arbitrary standards, is evident on Twitter and other social media sites. And it's a direct result of what has come to be a dearth of available options on account of forces dating back to the excision of men from communities of color during and after slavery.

OTHER WOMEN have rejected the idea of needing anyone, and of course that's seen as a rejection of traditional family life inside and outside the community. But being a single woman for longer or being a single parent isn't a failure on the part of women in these communities. Their choices are a reaction to the external pressure of white supremacy and the internal pressure of a form of feminism born in the crucible that is survival. The newer standards of expecting Black women to uphold traditional gender roles, to cater to and care for the men in their homes no matter how tired they might be from their own work, was intended as a way to reclaim masculinity lost to oppression. However, those standards not only carry all the historical baggage of sexism, they also ignore the ongoing impact of current events on the women being subjected to them. With all Black and Brown youth at risk of being profiled as criminals, all marginalized people likely to be treated with disrespect and, increasingly, dehumanization, the space to actually examine and correct these issues inside the community is limited. Pressure from outside increases pressure on the inside, Black women face one of the highest rates of intimate partner violence, and they are blamed for everything from lower marriage rates to high crime.

And yet the new Black patriarchy doesn't work to heal the community. For the boys who subscribe to it, their ideas of respect have become so skewed that they are killing or dying over the most ridiculous conflicts. Homicide rates have declined substantially in communities of color, but the rate of shootings is still catastrophic, with teens in particular facing the greatest levels of risk.

Tackling hypermasculinity and toxic masculinity is a key part of ending the present crisis of gun violence, but obviously that isn't the only crisis inside communities of color. It is a clear mistake to focus on only one aspect of the patriarchy without being willing to interrogate the ways that other forms influence the rates of violence and trauma marginalized women and girls in particular are facing.

The ways that boys and girls handle the trauma inflicted by exposure to racist patriarchal notions can be very different, but internal cultural expectations are often gendered in ways that can feel isolating for those who don't fit into the strictly defined lines that can be the only space that's left.

For girls of color, especially Black and Latinx girls, there's not only the issue of navigating the projected hypersexualization of their bodies and the assumptions that they are somehow destined to fail, there's also the expectation that they perform emotional and social labor at the expense of their own girlhood. Adultification (the racist practice of seeing children of color as significantly older than they are) removes the possibility of innocence from young girls, especially Black girls. It shows up in many facets; one of the most bizarre is perhaps the response of white *Hunger Games* fans to the death of the character Rue, played by Amandla Stenberg, in the movie. Instead of the deep grief that fans reported feeling while reading the book, seeing Rue on-screen as a visibly Black girl had many commenting that they felt nothing. Or that her death was less meaningful to them because Rue was being played by a Black girl.

Some fans of the movie tweeted things like "Awkward moment when Rue is some black girl and not the innocent blonde girl you picture," and "Why does Rue have to be black? Not gonna lie, kinda ruined the movie." Despite the character being described in the text as having dark brown skin. Even a fictional Black girl wasn't immune to racism.

Though the existence and consequences of adultification likely affect all communities of color, the research around this phenomenon has primarily centered around Black communities. A report released in 2017 by Georgetown Law's Center on Poverty and Inequality called *Girlhood Interrupted: The Erasure of Black Girls' Childhood* found that all of the 325 adults in the study felt that Black girls seemed older than white girls of the same age. It also found respondents believed Black girls needed less nurturing, protection, support, and comfort than white girls. Adults in the study from all backgrounds (75 percent of them white, 62 percent of them women) saw Black girls as more independent and more mature. They also assumed that Black girls knew more about adult topics and sex.

It's unlikely the respondents were conscious of why they felt the way they did, as unconscious bias is heavily informed by the messaging that we pick up from the world around us. From an outside perspective, it seems likely to me that their attitudes reflected a wider cultural message. Much like the people who responded so angrily to the character of Rue, they likely had never seen Black girls portrayed as innocent and thus did not ask themselves why they felt that innocence was beyond them. But older studies show that this is a common form of dehumanization experienced by Black children. And that it has negative effects on their experiences with authority figures, who are less inclined to protect them, nurture them, or help them achieve their goals.

And for the Black girls (and likely for the Brown girls who can't pass as white) the narratives around a lack of innocence also apply in their own neighborhoods. We know that even inside their communities, girls of color aren't always safe, that the patriarchy that positions them as prey can find fertile ground for such messaging everywhere. And then those girls face having their trauma ignored or minimized while the systems that are supposed to protect them sacrifice their safety for respectability—see any conversation about how a girl is "ruining" someone's life by reporting that they have sexually harassed or assaulted her. Sports star, cop, celebrity, or teacher, it doesn't really matter who the perpetrator is, as long as he's preying on girls who society sees as unworthy of protection. There's minimal discussion of the harm he's done to her, and the focus is on protecting his potential, his future, while hers is ignored.

Girls of color, especially Black girls, must deal with erasure and higher expectations, all while managing to fit in with their peers without running into the clutches of the school-to-prison pipeline or predators, or succumbing to the kinds of stressors that are common in households struggling with economic insecurity. Young girls are left to navigate the expectations of family, school, church, and the street alone.

Code-switching in these spaces is a key skill that not everyone can or will acquire. And the toll of not being adept at this skill plays out not only in how girls are treated by their peers but also in how they are treated by the systems they encounter. A girl who is seen as fitting into the patriarchy's preset mold of a "good girl," one who won't engage in any of that pesky interest in herself, her own goals and concerns, but who is instead seemingly willing to be directed, will often find herself offered more resources by teachers, employers, or other people with power to effect a positive change in her life. A counterpart who is messier, louder, and more invested in being true to herself and where she came from, no matter how much that self departs from accepted ideas of a "good girl," is unlikely to benefit from the same resources.

Girls in the hood must learn to present only the fraction of themselves deemed acceptable while also working twice as hard to get half as far in life. Media depictions of code-switching tend to center on external changes such as altering your speech and changing your hairstyle, makeup, and body language, but the reality is that code switching goes much deeper than that. Girls in the hood have to navigate stressors, bury traumas, and still carve out the space to be human. Their efforts to do so are often pathologized as ghetto or silly by people who are more concerned with respectability than anything else, even if they claim to want to help marginalized girls. When the girls who aren't middle class get colorful hairstyles, seek the pretty consumer goods that are on display, or act in ways that are even the slightest bit outside of "proper," they can find themselves on the wrong end of the systems they are still learning to navigate.

To listen to some feminist narratives about the hood is to be told that it is merely a place to escape, a situation where the girls and women who continue to live there have no voice of their own and need an outsider to speak for them. Take the 2014 video campaign by the anti–street harassment organization Hollaback! that showed a white woman walking around New York. When she was in the hood, it was portrayed as a place where men harass you. The campaign never engaged with the treatment that women similarly experience from white men, who are much more likely to exhibit violence toward white women, much less what a woman of color might experience in the hood or anywhere else. It's true that street harassment is more likely to happen in places where women are walking on a public sidewalk or using public transit, as opposed to insulated from the outside world in a private vehicle. However, that doesn't mean that the hood is the only place it happens, much less that the women who live there need a white savior to step in for them.

Narratives like the one presented in the Hollaback! campaign video are a gross oversimplification of the complex problem of how the patriarchy at large teaches the world to ignore marginalized women, who often have the most scathing critiques and the most cogent analysis of reality. In many ways, the world is not reverting to earlier patterns; it is simply broadening a cycle that some communities have always faced. The patriarchy isn't dead, nor is it the same everywhere, and calling for solutions without addressing the impact of class and race evades the real problem. As a society, we face a vicious tangle of income inequality exacerbated by unchecked bigotry that has been allowed to seep into every community.

But for girls raised in areas of concentrated poverty, amid oppression aided and abetted by a police culture that prioritizes racial profiling and violent constraint over protection, their focus has to be survival. They are fighting to save not only themselves but also their communities, to preserve the parts of their cultures that they hold dear without being drowned in the flawed fundamentalism that is the narrow range of femininity available to them. They already know that respectability cannot save them because it can't save anyone, and now they are figuring out how to cope with the trauma internally and with a world that treats them with such disrespect and disdain. They have to find inspiration in the people who make it out—not necessarily out of the hood itself, but out of the cycle of trauma wrought by poverty and oppression. The hood is still home, but they have to look beyond the troubled streets they are on every day and see themselves as worthy of saving.

Finding or creating good programs for girls and young women in these communities isn't always easy, but the resiliency of these girls is sometimes amazing. They create a way out of no way on their own, or with the help of their parents whenever possible. If you asked working-class moms in these neighborhoods, many would say that girls are most at risk, and yet they are among the worst resourced. Hastily expanded intervention programs cover topics ranging from suicide to self-harm in an attempt to include girls, but perhaps not enough to really focus on their needs. Courses on healthy relationships cover street and gang connections alongside the ways to spot abusive partners and improve self-esteem, but the programs don't center on what the girls might want or need for themselves. Instead of treating them as self-determining agents in their own lives, they treat the girls as only capable of responding to what is happening around them.

My focus on girls is not to the exclusion of LGBTQIA youth, who are no more insulated from the harm that comes from toxic masculinity. On the contrary, it greatly contributes to their heightened risk factors and positions LGBTQIA youth on the outskirts of the cisgender heteronormative communities they often inhabit. Literally and figuratively, toxic masculinity is killing them. Entitlement, intolerance, homophobia, misogyny, aggression, and sexual violence inside and outside marginalized communities are the antisocial behaviors that patriarchal systems create. There can be no doubt that patriarchal systems have oppressed, terrorized, and abused everyone. As part of working toward a society that will be beneficial for all, marginalized communities need to do more internal work to address these behaviors and work together to undo the harm that has been done. But toxic masculinity isn't just a problem in low-income communities, which are no more homophobic or intolerant or sexually violent than communities with higher socioeconomic standing. There's not a clearly marked boundary between safe and unsafe that can be drawn along color or class lines.

Toxic narratives about masculinity are blurring the lines between sexual violence, misogyny, and homophobia with the more benign desires of being strong and courageous, creating a system that rewards prejudiced attitudes at the same time it undermines more positive ones. The inheritance of a colonialist patriarchy has meant that many communities struggle to recover the good in traditional characteristics of their culture's attitudes around gender. The absence of precolonial knowledge that recognizes the spectrum of gender can do as much harm as a culture enforcing norms on those for whom they do not fit.

Under the "protective" narratives of the patriarchal structures that fill our society, there's always room for toxic masculinity to manifest. And the fundamental problems of sexism, racism, and homophobia are deeply intertwined with what we think of as more positive masculine behaviors. Too often comments that promote toxic masculinity are masked in language that valorizes dangerous mentalities. Far too often those in relationships with men are told that they need to be submissive, to learn how to hold a man down no matter what, to be understanding and patient despite red flags ranging from cheating to outright abuse. Calling these things out is necessary, albeit difficult to do when a community is figuring out not just how to dismantle patriarchal structures but also how to replace them. And replacing them will benefit everyone, making it easier to confront internalized homophobia and transphobia that is rooted in the devaluation of women and girls. We have to work toward equity within and without.

Ultimately there is one long-term, fundamental change that can come only from within marginalized communities: a reduction in the number of structures that seek to mimic instead of challenge patriarchal narratives. Instead of long-winded screeds from respectability-obsessed authority figures, ready to lay all sins on the doorstep of those born to single, usually poor women, hood feminists would talk about the harm done by those more interested in sustaining gender roles than in solving problems ranging from poverty to child abuse. Feminism needs to create room for marginalized communities to talk about more than reactions to educational failures and delinquency, and instead talk about what can be done to create a space for kids of color to thrive. We need to circumvent the patriarchal influences in our lives, especially among boys, who often end up joining gangs in order to find a level of respect and love that they are missing. We must continue to push for an egalitarian society in which women and girls have every opportunity afforded men and boys and are free from violence.

Despite white feminist narratives to the contrary, there is no absence of feminism inside Islam, the Black church, or any other community. The women inside those communities are doing the hard and necessary work; they don't need white saviors, and they don't need to structure their feminism to look like anyone else's. They just need to not have to constantly combat the white supremacist patriarchy from the outside while they work inside their communities.

We can't sacrifice the futures of girls and femmes to preserve the futures of young toxic men or the institutions that made them possible. Nor can we pretend that feminism is fracturing our communities. It's the patriarchy; it's always the patriarchy. But the patriarchy has more heads than the Hydra and must be tackled from all sides.

If mainstream white feminism wants something to do, wants to help, this is one area where it is important to step back, to wait to be invited in. If no invitation is forthcoming? Well, you can always challenge the white patriarchy. There's always space to combat the prison industrial complex, to advocate for the reduction of incarceration as a solution for societal concerns. There's space to limit the harm done to marginalized communities without intruding on the internal work that insiders can and must do. And that space can operate from the outside.

HOW TO WRITE ABOUT
BLACK WOMEN

First, state your credentials. It's okay to be a woman, but not a Black woman. Their lived experiences are immaterial and can be dismissed as merely anecdotal. Make it clear that you are not racist or sexist, you are merely concerned about their plight. What plight? Well, pick one. Or several. Marriage, children, lack of either, too much education, not enough education, welfare, whatever you think will sell. It only matters that you highlight their troublesome natures. Whatever it is, you must be sure to make it clear that they aren't like other women. They are failing to perform in some way that affects the whole of society, even if you can't quite explain how or why their personal lives are public property. Further, rely heavily on the idea of research that shows the problem is a problem. Never mention exactly when that research was done, or who were the subjects of it. Too much context may unnecessarily complicate the conversation. And those pesky facts might get in the way of your ultimate goal.

Utilize stereotypes whenever possible, preferably ones that tie into the Mammy, Jezebel, or Sapphire tropes. Describe Black women in ways that play up their sexuality and remove their humanity. After all they are Other, so their skin is a foodstuff, the space between their thighs is mysterious, and they have never, ever been innocent. No need to mention virginity or purity; even when speaking of Black female infants, your focus must be on their sexuality. If you are speaking of Black mothers, make it clear that they need guidance, financial support, or salvation. What salvation? Well, that all depends on whether they work too little and thus are on welfare, or work too much and thus are neglecting their children. There is no point at which they can balance work and family, because, again, they are Other and that is not possible for them. They are emasculating and thus unworthy of relationships, or they are the key to being masculine with their all-knowing sexuality that is present from birth. Un-rapeable, they can be trusted to raise any children but their own and are sexually available until they become sexless.

They exist to be support systems, whether for men of all colors or women of every color but black. No need to mention their needs, hopes, dreams, or concerns. They have none, even if they do occasionally speak of themselves as real people with feelings. Their voices are too loud, too uneducated, or simply too aggressive. They are always angry about something, but their feelings aren't real, so they don't matter. Be sure to specify how reasonable you are in the face of their unreasonable behavior. Write of how you studied them at a safe distance, while proclaiming that some of your closest friends are Black women. No need to know anything about those close friends but their names, since all that matters is that you have them as proof that you know your subject and are not racist or sexist.

Contrast them with women of other races, always making sure to highlight that other women are real women, while Black women are simply Black. Feel free to make blanket statements about their religious beliefs, educational levels, income levels, and family dynamics. All of it is true because you say it is, and you are the expert in Black women, not any actual Black women. If they are offended by your words, remind them of your credentials and refuse to engage in a conversation with them until they can be less emotional. Point to their tone as a reason to doubt the veracity of their experiences. After all, they are only Black women and thus they know nothing, own nothing, and are worth nothing but what you say they are.

WHAT STARTED as an internal philosophy post-slavery to "uplift the race" by correcting the "bad" traits of poor and working-class Black people has now evolved into one of the hallmarks of what is expected of Black American women. Propriety has become a governing philosophy in media, the workplace, and the academy, especially for Black women as they age. It is a societal expectation that centers on managing the behavior of Black people, largely Black women, who have otherwise been neglected in a society that only wants to offer opportunity to those who have been approved by gatekeepers.

Respectability depends on acceptably performing gender and

sexuality in ways that don't threaten traditional ideas of masculinity. In order to maintain their social and economic status, Black women are expected to manage their identities and sexual reputations in order to fit into a mixture of virgin and vixen constructs. Black women who attempt to craft an image of innocence may receive slightly more sympathy and thus better opportunities, but their ability to adhere to that image is tenuous.

Respectability politics are really about controlling group behavior with designations of appropriate or inappropriate behavior rooted in structural inequality. Gatekeepers of respectability push dominant narratives but don't necessarily understand where their ideas of what is respectable come from, or how much of it is about mimicry and not innate value. The structure of respectability requires adherence, not autonomy, and relies on dominant norms to create a hierarchy of privilege inside marginalized communities.

In an era marked by rising inequality and declining economic mobility for Black Americans, the modern version of the politics of respectability works to accommodate misogynoir. *Misogynoir* is a term coined by queer Black feminist professor Moya Bailey to describe the specific misogyny directed toward Black women in American visual and popular culture because of their race and gender. Self-care and self-correction are framed as strategies to lift poor Black women out of the hood by preparing them to participate in an economy that will demand respectability as a key part of being able to access even the least desirable jobs. In this way, respectability acts to simultaneously enable and limit the scope of opportunities for communities to thrive.

We have tied concepts like "lift as we climb" (coined after the Civil War to describe the idea that successful Black people had a duty to help those behind them) so deeply to what we present to the outside world that we don't even realize that working to prove to white America that Black people are worthy of full citizenship is ultimately a losing proposition. Any system that ties our rights to getting the entire Black community to assimilate isn't interested in equality, much less equity. Modern politics of respectability have gone a step further, demanding that Black people pull themselves up by imaginary bootstraps in order to be found worthy.

Inherent in the ideology of respectability, like most strategies for progress that fail to confront the impact of anti-Blackness, becoming a gatekeeper isn't the road to freedom for anyone. This is an issue that largely played out away from the gaze of white America. But now that some Black Americans have achieved a measure of success that renders them hypervisible in ways that make them part of the mainstream elite in media, business, politics, and the academy, respectability politics influence what is perceived as acceptable within the official boundaries of the mainstream. Respectability-focused gatekeepers are shaping who gets to have opinions that inform policies on what should and should not be available to the poorest Black communities.

Respectability politics have become de facto rules for marginalized people to follow in order to be respected in mainstream culture, but they reflect antiquated ideals set up by white supremacy. The depiction of the cultures that Black Americans create in low-income areas like the hood as ghetto or ratchet has very little to do with any real interest in their success, and everything to do with creating a series of hoops and obstacles to arbitrarily impede the progress of those with the fewest resources.

Overwhelmingly, respectability is financially and emotionally expensive. Like code-switching, it requires fundamental changes in how you present yourself. But there aren't just specific speech patterns that are changed in the moment; instead there's a nonstop remodeling of body language, wardrobe, and hairstyles so as to be seen as nonthreatening, engaged, and somehow ready to join the broader world. In many ways, respectability politics treat assimilation and accommodation as mandatory. Yet we know that respectability comes with no guarantees. The demand is that Black women police their appearances, speech, and sexuality. There's a cultural pressure to be an upstanding Black woman, to avoid any behavior that makes Black women "look bad." We are expected to constantly adjust our own behavior to avoid the racist, classist, and sexist stereotypes other people might assign to us.

But while we put this pressure on each other and ourselves, it does little to stop the impact of racism. Sure, it makes us feel like we have slightly more control when we know the ultimate culprit is racism and the work of dismantling it can't be done by us. But when Black women internalize the standards set by racism and hold ourselves to oppressive standards, we create a self-replicating schism inside our own communities. We pretend that the problem is the girls with the hoop earrings and the fishnets; we hop on a bandwagon of venerating standard English over African American Vernacular English, only to end up angry that even as it is derided, everyone else feels free to capitalize on it. We write classism into our own communities, standing in the way of the smart and the talented if they can't code-switch. We enforce our oppression on a micro level and dabble in the culture, but refuse to defend those who create and contribute to it unless they are part of the lucky few who get famous.

Respectability politics are, at their core, an easy way to avoid engaging with history and current events. If we admit that Blackness comes in many forms, that our culture is glorious and worthwhile, then we also have to face the fact that we will never be able to achieve this mythical space where color doesn't matter, where our class and culture is respected. We want a route to undo the impact of history and it simply doesn't exist.

We point to the suits and ties and dresses worn during the civil rights movement and ignore that the people in them were still beaten, still arrested, still lynched. We sneer at the innovations in the hood until we see them on the right celebrities. We adore the idea of a fierce Black girl who fights back, but we penalize her as soon as she does it.

We love a Black accent on everyone but Black women. Mind you, there is absolutely nothing wrong with sounding Black except that in a culture where respectability politics mean that whiteness is rendered as normative, a Black girl who speaks with a "blaccent" is judged as less valuable and less intelligent. Code-switching elders teach us to make calls with our best "white girl" voice, but for those who can't manage to mimic that speech pattern, or who can't maintain it, that accent means the loss of opportunities.

We treat speaking in African American Vernacular English in much the same American-centric way that we treat people who can't speak English. We judge them when they appear on TV as victims of brutality from the state; we bemoan the proliferation of more casual language rooted in slang from marginalized communities, even though we know all language is a human construct and none of it is more valid than any other.

When we carry these respectability politics into mainstream spaces, we don't just exercise them against Black women—though they are the most likely to be impacted—we also see them used against other communities. Suddenly the question of who is closest to whiteness gets even more complicated. Xenophobia, Islamophobia, and more can be interwoven with respectability narratives to punish anyone for almost anything, from speaking with a Spanish accent to wearing a hijab to preferring to spend more time with coworkers of color. And in feminist spaces, the expectations of who will be heard, of who will have the agency, the autonomy, and the respect, is heavily informed by the lens of respectability.

It is that reliance on respectability that allows mainstream feminism to ignore those who can't speak in the "tone" that centers on the comfort of whiteness. The tone policing of respectability ensures that the fight for equality becomes the responsibility of the oppressed. It alleviates the responsibility of the powerful and the privileged to listen and to learn. It protects privilege by forcing marginalized people to calmly respond to injustice or risk their feelings being a barrier to resources. It renders even the expression of feminist issues an exercise in navigating privilege, in having to earn your way to be able to critique, express anger or fear, or even ask for help. And it means that white-centered expectations of politeness, of muted emotions, are projected onto the righteous anger and sometimes grief of women of color. Respectability requires a form of restrained, emotionally neutral politeness that is completely at odds with any concept of normal human emotions.

The emotional labor required to be respectable, to never ruffle anyone's feathers, to not get angry enough to challenge much less confront those who might have harmed you, is incredibly onerous precisely because it is so dehumanizing. Respectability requires not just a stiff upper lip, but a burying of yourself inside your own flesh in order to be able to maintain the necessary facade. It requires erasing your memory of how it felt to be hungry, cold, scared, and so on until all that is left is a placid surface to mask the raging maelstrom underneath. We talk about stress and illness, but the stress of respectability is unparalleled. You muffle yourself over and over, until the screaming is in your veins, in your high blood pressure and lower life expectancy. And then as you look around, you realize that you didn't even get the respect, the validation, or the comfort that you thought was waiting on the other side. You've pulled away from the messy, loud, emotional spaces that represent the less respectable side of you and your culture, but at what cost?

Imagining a new and less problematic future for marginalized communities means letting go of every aspect of white supremacy. It means embracing Blackness in all its forms and doing the hard work of rooting out the classist narratives around it. It means doing the listening and the learning that each one of us needs in order to be accountable. We have to stop maintaining the status quo and toxic hierarchies of respectability. We must understand that our involvement in this structure is a problem, whether we were conscious of it or not in the past; we know now and we need to be willing to change our standards and expectations. As feminists we need to take critical, radical measures in listening to women in the poorest communities about what they want and need instead of projecting narratives of ignorance onto them. We must work to unlearn the harmful narratives we've been taught and that we created in response to white supremacy.

The labor (physical and emotional) of low-income women is often abused and unappreciated. We are constantly watching them struggle and pretending it is voluntary and not a result of a system upheld by a powerful few that is fundamentally anti-Black and patriarchal. As people of color, we ignore parts of ourselves routinely to be able to compete in this structure, and then we disdain them when we see them in others. On the one hand, as a society, we worship Black cool, adore it, and wallow in its impact. On the other, people who are ostensibly socially and politically aware/woke are often disappointed that the creators of the cool don't know as much as a sociology professor, or aren't as educated in the mechanisms of oppression—again, as an academic might be—all while ignoring the oppression that we enable via classism. I'm not arguing that civic knowledge needs to be dumbed down, or spoon-fed to the creators of Black cool, but rather that the assumption that the learning curve to a woke mentality is short for everyone is a flawed assumption. In reality, some of the best-known creators of Black cool are gaining access to knowledge while they are in the public eye.

As a society, when homophobia and transphobia are espoused by hip-hop artists, country musicians, or other popular media, we tend to pretend that the dangers faced by LGBTQIA people only come from the disadvantaged. We assert that any real danger is from those whose upbringing in the hood or hills limited their exposure to people who aren't straight or cisgender. But if we're being honest, the people most addicted to maintaining the status quo are those who reap the greatest rewards. It's not that there is no bigotry in the hood, but much of it comes in from institutions and ends up being transmitted in media. Churches, politicians, even some educational institutions teach hate and normalize it long before it ends up in a song lyric or being parroted in an interview by a newly famous sixteen-year-old. In that way the hood is a reflection of the wider world. We don't have bigotry by accident; it's built and sustained by the same cultural institutions we're taught to revere.

We cannot keep sustaining a system of gatekeeping that privileges a very few at the expense of the majority. We embraced the logic of putting whiteness on a pedestal and then forgot that the traditional behaviors it demanded had nothing to do with us, and everything to do with controlling us. Feminism needs to learn to listen to the voices on the front lines, to accept that the gatekeepers don't know everything and in fact largely lack the lived experience to relate to those they claim to represent. We need to take a hard look at ourselves and ask why we value the behaviors that don't accomplish anything of note, instead of interrogating them.

We need to let go of respectability politics and understand that whiteness as a construct will never approve of us, and that the approval of white supremacy is nothing that we or any community should be seeking. We have to be willing to embrace the full autonomy of people who are less privileged and understand that equity means making access to opportunity easier, not deciding what opportunities they deserve. We need to be less concerned with appearance and more concerned with solutions.

We have to change how we talk about Blackness, about poverty, about the women who inhabit those spaces where access and opportunity rarely intersect. We have to be ready to listen to the girls and women who are still there, and not just the ones who were able to get out. We have to remember that respectability is the poisoned soil white supremacy gave us, not the hood, not being ghetto or ratchet. We have to be willing to regularly put the needs and concerns of those with the least before our comfort. We were taught to fear the impact of rejection by whiteness, to embrace their standards without giving much thought to the impact on our own well-being or that of our communities. We have to break down this conditioning, have to ask ourselves why we're more concerned with how we are received by the white supremacist patriarchy than we are with protecting ourselves.

The hood is my home, and always will be, but I am deeply aware of the way that my privilege in being able to code-switch and to see and mimic middle-class manners has given me access.

I'm not above admitting I have my own biases when it comes to criticizing views I strongly disagree with. But I always want to be able to look at myself in the mirror and know that I didn't disrespect the sacrifices that made it possible for me to be where I am now. I know the extent of the damage respectability narratives have inflicted on our movements, on our communities, and on our psyches.

There's no doubt that the white supremacist patriarchy needs to be dismantled, but we can't pretend that classism inside the Black community isn't also a major problem. We need to unpack what it means to be a gatekeeper, to be willing to call for the uprooting of bigotry, but not face the ways it has influenced our narratives. We have to fight our own battles, and handle our own unpacking process, not just hope that getting rid of the overarching problem will get rid of all the problems. Being Black and being a feminist are not mutually exclusive; when I say "we," I mean the Black community as a whole and Black feminists in particular, because we are sometimes best equipped to access resources that can benefit everyone.

The traumas of the past are woven into the fabric of our coping mechanisms. We have to create new ones that don't rely on perfectly packaged responses or ways to change ourselves to be accepted. I know we can come to a place where we embrace differences instead of pretending that freedom comes from erasing them.

PRETTY FOR A . . .

I don't actually know who my biological father is, but presumably, like every Black American descended from enslaved people, there's some white hanging around in his family tree. There definitely is some white and Indigenous ancestry hanging around in my maternal line. Depending on if you're my grandmother's side (largely shrouded in secrecy) or my grandfather's (hello genealogy obsession, complete with records), the amounts of other ancestries vary. We're Black with some sprinkles of Irish that might explain the freckles and occasional outbursts of red hair, but none of us have ever had to consider passing as anything else, so the fact of so much internal ranking based on skin tone and hair texture in my family is more than a little bizarre sometimes, especially since I'm the family yeti. I'm the tall one, broad shouldered, and built like I came here to box. Think Serena Williams with less money and athletic prowess, but still more muscular than anything else. My cousins, on the other hand, are short, fine boned, with the narrow shoulders that you would expect from women that tiny. The one thing we all share is curves. Theirs always looked like they fit right, while mine were the physical equivalent of press-on nails until weight lifting took me from being chronically underweight to finally fitting this frame.

As I transitioned from Not-Quite-Yellow Awkward to Pretty for a Black Girl, I discovered that beauty aesthetics inside my community weren't the only place I could feel alienated. I'm brown skinned, what some folks would call medium toned, so I largely sit on the outskirts of any major colorism debate. But I have a wide nose and full lips, and a big ass, which means that in any conversation about white-centric beauty aesthetics, I have the features that are revered or reviled depending on who's talking. When I was a teenager with the worst taste in white boys, I dated the kind of men who would say things like "You're pretty for a Black girl," and I'd chalk it up to ignorance instead of malice. Backhanded compliments were still better than no compliments, in my mind. I was a fool. A fool with low self-esteem, but still a fool.

I was an astonishingly awkward-looking child. If you were feeling generous and moderately poetic you could have called me fey. Proportions were not on my side. I didn't grow into my head until I was twelve; I wasn't cute, I was just lighter skinned than some of my maternal cousins. What I did have on my side, in the color-struck narratives that came from some family members, was my light skin. I didn't have "good hair," but I was lighter skinned than most of Mom's side of the family, and as far as they were concerned, that was something of a boon for an otherwise odd-looking child. One of my aunts tried to solve the problem of my hair by taking me to a kitchen beautician who put a lye relaxer on my head when I was three. In a very few minutes I was crying, bleeding, and burned. It's one of my earliest memories, and I can't say that I completely understood what had happened to me.

Even before the perm that burned me, the few pictures I've seen of me as a toddler make it clear that my family always did something to tame my hair. No wild-haired pictures of a running baby with an Afro. I can't remember one time when my hair was allowed to just be the way it grew out of my head. For years after the relaxer incident, Grandmother took me to the salon every two weeks like clockwork. She meant well, but she had a whole lot of internalized issues around hair and skin color that meant I didn't see myself with natural hair until I was seventeen. By then I had tried no-lye relaxers, applied heat daily, and generally battered my hair until it was damaged. It was around then that I started trying to rebel against that "Natural is not good enough" aesthetic.

When I first tried to go natural, it was early 1994 or thereabouts, and I had no idea how to take care of my hair. This was well before YouTube gurus or the wealth of easy-to-find products designed for my hair texture. I tried using the existing products, but I had no idea what I was doing with my hair and it showed. I eventually caved under the pressure from family members to style it differently and got it relaxed again after about a year. Being in charge of my own hair meant that I could minimize how many times a year I got a relaxer, and for the next thirteen years, my hair veered wildly from perfectly coiffed to mostly new growth. Along the way, I came to understand that my hair grows rapidly, and styles that rely on changing texture require a level of upkeep that I am not willing to do. In 2005, while pregnant with my youngest son, I got tired of my hair. Just absolutely fed up with the need to sit in a shop, to wrap it or flat-iron it or whatever. So, I shaved my head. Well, I cut off all my hair, and my husband walked in on his five-months-pregnant wife with scissors and stepped in to do the actual shaving.

Post-chop (after the initial shock) I started learning how to deal with it. And for a long time, while it was growing out, I wasn't entirely sold on being natural. Mostly I was convinced that I had consigned myself to looking unfortunate for some months. Because of how I was raised, I used to be one of those Black women who thought natural hair looked a mess. Then I started growing up and really paying attention to what well-maintained natural styles looked like on friends and neighbors. And over time I started wishing I could wear a twist out or puffs. I had no idea how to really do my hair. None.

Because I grew up going to beauty salons where my hair was pressed bone straight, braided, or relaxed, my relationship with it was casual. I could wash it, blow-dry it, and flat-iron it, but actually care for it? Not so much. When it got long enough for me to want to style it, I had to rely on the magic of YouTube channels "recommended by friends." And the more I learned, the more I liked having natural hair. Because suddenly, doing my hair didn't have to involve any pain. None. And some of you

reading this are probably thinking, "Why the hell do Black women do that if it hurts?" and there's a whole list of answers to
that question that range from preferences, to not being able to
be employed without straightened hair, to internalized racism.

Every time I need to wash and twist my hair, I gripe about it.
Natural hair is work even with locs, but for me, in some ways it
feels like a form of self-care. It's easier for me than wearing my
hair loose because detangling is an exercise in muscle failure.
But texturism (the valuing of certain textures of hair above others) in the natural hair community is rampant. In many ways it
is an outgrowth of the same colorism that made my family see
me as moderately attractive even when I was mostly eyes and
legs and mouth.

For a time, I was enamored with the privileges that pretty
gives you, even when you aren't necessarily inside the lines of a
white beauty aesthetic. Going from being an awkward child to a
relatively attractive young woman changed my life in a lot of
positive ways. Not just in terms of male attention, though that
was flattering at first, but people were more accommodating at
every turn. Applying for my first job as a mall survey person?
Being attractive was on the unspoken list of requirements. Getting my lunch in the food court? Chances were good that if the
person at the register was a guy I wasn't paying for my fries.

It was great for my burgeoning self-esteem, though I can't
say that it came without a price. In between bouts of promiscuity (that were about my ego and my ownership of my sexuality)
I learned to tune out street harassment, to fend off the wander-
ing hands of "friendly" men who just wanted a hug. I even learned

that other women weren't the enemy or the competition no matter what happened with the guys I did like, or the ones I didn't. But what I am still learning is how much of what I do is about what I want versus the ways that the outside world mandates what constitutes attractiveness.

In order to be pretty in a white-centered aesthetic or in a Black one you have to look as if you spend at least some time in the beauty parlor, or at least with a good kitchen beautician. Even though the broader societal expectations around beauty for women prioritize things like an hourglass figure, smooth, clear skin, and symmetrical features, there are some distinct differences based on your proximity to whiteness in terms of skin color, hair texture, and body type. Having hair that is not styled well, clothes that aren't flattering, and so on can undermine your chances at success. While a messy bun might be considered sloppy chic for white girls, any hint that a Black woman has failed to put effort into her appearance is met with ardent disapproval both inside her community and outside it. Viewer backlash to Gabby Douglas sweating out her edges at the Olympics filled the news cycle for days; even Blue Ivy's hair has been critiqued repeatedly. Five minutes after it was confirmed that (now Duchess) Meghan Markle was dating Prince Harry, white women rushed to criticize her hair. Tossing aside any awareness that a biracial woman might have different hair-care needs, they focused on her hair's failure to match that of her new white sister-in-law, Duchess Catherine.

Racism in beauty aesthetics doesn't mean that women don't still benefit from the privilege their looks afford them, but it shows how tenuous that privilege can be, especially once you factor in the reality that it is not permanent. And while there's really no actual safety in pretty, it can feel less fraught than being unattractive.

One of my biggest lessons in the way that being attractive can cut against you was when I was sexually harassed at work. Not that harassment is a problem related to attractiveness, but the responses to it are often filtered through a lens of victim-blaming rhetoric around looks. I reported it the first time; it happened again; I reported it again. Finally, thankfully the harassment stopped, possibly because I threatened a measure of bodily harm. In the midst of the cycle of harassment I got pulled into the office of a white female supervisor so she could warn me about smiling so much. She said, "You're a pretty girl, but you're too friendly, and the way you dress..." She trailed off and looked me up and down, her disapproval very clear. I was wearing a long-sleeved sweater dress, leggings, and boots because it was January in Chicago and professional dress for work only offers so many options. There wasn't much I could wear that would hide my curves, and apparently being covered from my neck to my toes still wasn't enough.

Meanwhile I was supposed to have been flattered by the attentions of men in whom I had no interest. Because why else did I wear dresses that fit? And why wasn't I flattered when they told me they weren't usually interested in Black women, but I was the exception? Being harassed made me feel dirty and scared, but the narrative assigned to me from the outside was that I was supposed to not only feel flattered but also have no expectation of respect or safety at work or anywhere else. It's amazing what those "compliments" will teach you once you're past the point of finding validation in them. Turns out back-handed compliments are offensive and ugly. Who knew?

Once I was able to see the trap in "pretty for a Black girl" and in getting hung up on the privileges of pretty, I started to really shift how I looked at myself and the world around me. As my relationship with my body and my hair improved, I could also see the trap in a single beauty aesthetic or in any aesthetic that hinged on proximity to whiteness. But my personal journey doesn't resolve the larger issues of colorism in America or anywhere else in the world. That old rhyme about whose skin color was accept-able still applies:

> If you're black, stay back;
> If you're brown, stick around;
> If you're yellow, you're mellow;
> If you're white, you're all right.

Not only does the rhyme explain colorism, it also continues to inform the ways that society views people. And it's so insidi-ous that often people perpetuate it without really thinking about what they are doing or why. When the sequel to *Wreck-It Ralph* was announced, screen shots of a meeting between the Disney princesses included Princess Tiana, but not the darker-skinned, wide-nosed version so familiar from her own movie. No, this version had a narrow nose, hair that looked nothing like an Afro texture, and much lighter skin. Why? Because the artists didn't think about what it would mean to erase those features. While we know that colorism refers to discrimination based on skin color and that it disadvantages dark-skinned people while privileging those with lighter skin, it is about more than just beauty aesthetics. Having darker skin is linked to lower job prospects, difficulty getting promoted into high-level positions, lower marriage rates, higher rates of arrest, and longer prison terms. As a society we tend to erase dark-skinned people and even punish them for existing.

Colorism has existed for centuries, in multiple cultures, and Black Americans are not the only community that places a higher or lower value on someone based on how light or dark that person's skin is. Colorism is a global issue found in Latin America, East and Southeast Asia, the Caribbean, and Africa. Here in the United States, because we are such a diverse population it is possible to experience privilege based on skin color inside your community and still experience oppression outside it.

In the United States, Latin America, the Caribbean, and Africa, colorism has roots in colonialism and slavery, but in some cultures, it predates any contact with European beauty ideals and may be more related to class than to white supremacy. Laborers tanned as they worked outdoors, while the privileged had lighter complexions because they were inside. Socially, dark skin became associated with poverty and light skin with the aristocracy. Today, the premium on light skin in parts of Asia is likely tangled up with this history, along with cultural influences of the Western world that also positioned "rednecks" at the lower end of the social strata of whiteness for similar reasons.

Colorism is a cultural institution that has skewed access to opportunity by consistently placing those with lighter skin in positions of privilege. This is why things like paper bag tests and comb tests proliferated in some parts of higher-income Black communities. For the paper bag test, a paper bag would be held against your skin and if you were darker than the bag, you weren't admitted to a nightclub, a fraternity, or sometimes even a church. The comb test functioned in a similar manner: if you couldn't pass a fine-tooth comb through your hair, then you were locked out of certain social circles. Even now, if you watch the "natural hair gurus" who become influencers and make a significant amount of income, they tend to be lighter skinned with a looser curl pattern.

And colorism means that lighter skin yields real-world advantages in every community. Campaigns for skin-bleaching products make a point of highlighting lighter skin being key not just to higher incomes, but to a better love life. As a result, lighter skin is so coveted that bleaching creams continue to be bestsellers in the United States, Asia, and other nations despite evidence of mercury poisoning, skin damage, and liver and other organ malfunctions. For many communities the potential rewards outweigh the risks because of societal pressure.

Similarly, looser hair texture is associated with success to the point that businesses and schools feel free to limit access based on it. Recently the US Eleventh Circuit Court ruled that discriminating against people with locs isn't discrimination because hair texture is a mutable characteristic and thus isn't a protected status, but statistically speaking those most likely to wear the style are of African descent, and race is a protected category under current laws against discrimination.

Colorism and texturism play out in so-called feminist spaces too. We already know that mainstream feminism isn't immune to the prejudices attached to certain skin colors. And for some white women who might be unremarkable in majority white communities, moving into communities of color via spray-on tans, appropriating hairstyles like box braids, or even claiming to "feel Black" à la Rachel Dolezal (a white woman who continues to claim a right to identify as a Black woman despite having two white parents) can mean that they get to benefit from a colorist beauty standard without ever having to engage with the harm it does.

Despite claims to mean no harm, we all know that skin color continues to serve as the most obvious criterion in determining how a person will be treated. In America and around the world, because of deeply entrenched racism and anti-Blackness, we know that dark skin is demonized and light skin is generally prized. So it serves no one to feign ignorance of what it means to capitalize on fetishization and exoticism without doing anything to combat the problems most likely to be faced by those who are disadvantaged by these standards.

While Black feminism has been combating colorism for decades with campaigns against skin bleaching, pushing for better media representation of darker-skinned girls and women, and pushing the idea of beauty aesthetics that don't center on whiteness, it's not just a Black feminist issue. If we want to raise an empowered next generation of Black and Brown girls who can love themselves, love one another, and change the world, we need mainstream feminism to start calling out colorism and addressing it.

We know that white supremacist narratives around skin color have not just fueled self-hatred, depression, and anxiety for girls and women of color, they have also been used to justify white fragility narratives that contribute to the privileging of white women's tears over the lives of women of color. Exotification isn't freedom; any feminism that hinges on the fetishization of the beauty of women of color is toxic. In a media culture where even a Disney princess is subject to colorism, you have to ask why so many mainstream feminist narratives are more likely to call a dark-skinned woman powerful and not beautiful.

And then there's the questions of size, of disability, of the ways that some body types are seen as more valuable than others. There's a narrative that because Black women consistently report having higher self-esteem than white or Latina women, that means they don't need the care or concern around beauty that other women do. But that higher level of self-esteem is built across time inside our communities, and not every girl gets the support that she needs to combat a culture that says her body is always going to be wrong.

It's easy to say that beauty standards are superficial and unimportant when your skin color safely positions you at the top of someone's beauty aesthetic. But, like everything else, beauty is political. Embracing as beautiful a body that isn't adjacent to whiteness is an act of resistance, a way to keep alive the culture and community that colonialism and imperialism were attempting to crush.

Of course, pretty can be a privilege, but how that privilege functions varies wildly based on race. The same metric that might position a beautiful white woman as someone worthy of adoration or respect can be twisted to mean that a darker-skinned woman with similar features is read as not only sexually available but outright obscene simply for existing in public. It's the proverbial tightrope over a snake pit.

Being taught you're strong, you're beautiful, you're smart, you're enough is a generational defense mechanism against discrimination. Even when the confidence isn't really felt, you know that the more confident you appear, the better equipped you'll be to deal with racism. As a result, a premium is placed on appearance. Body positivity originated in the Black community because skin shade, size, body type, and visible disabilities rendered many in the community outsiders even in spaces that were intended to be affirming. Even now beauty is complicated by class, the quality of hair purchased for a weave, the brand of clothes that can be afforded—these are all markers that signal whether your body has a right to be in the space it is occupying. And even if all the trappings are correct, there's still the question of how your features may be commodified and presented as attractive on every body but the one you're in when you're not white.

The fad of white women being praised for altering their bodies, plumping their lips, and tanning their skin will fade. This dabbling in an exotic identity will disappear, but for dark-skinned women their oppression will remain largely unchanged, unless the racism and colorism in beauty culture and our broader culture is challenged.

Pretty comes with privileges, and when one's health, wealth, and opportunity for success in this country are impacted by looks, by the color of your skin, and by the texture of your hair, who gets to define pretty matters. Colorism is so deeply ingrained in the fabric of this nation that we are all implicated in its impact for good or for ill. The pervasive color hierarchy is one that many communities are facing without a true mechanism to end it, as long as our cultures are interconnected, and ultimately, we need intra-racial and interracial solutions. We need cross-cultural dialogue about the impact of colorism before we can even begin to move on to really creating better, healthier beauty aesthetics.

Mainstream feminist engagement with beauty culture often centers on the male gaze and its impact, but that's not the only toxic component. The ways that being white, cis, slim, and able-bodied are valorized must be addressed. As a movement feminism needs to be willing to move the needle, to interrogate the ways that it engages in colorist hierarchies internally. It needs to be open to asking why so many white feminists are willing to leave these problems to be solved by feminists of color. Equity in beauty culture requires investment from all sides, not just those who are least likely to have the power and privilege to make the most lasting change.

BLACK GIRLS DON'T
HAVE EATING DISORDERS

I had an eating disorder in high school. I was always skinny, and I genuinely think my weight loss wasn't really noticeable at first, especially because I had mastered all of the seemingly healthy eating tricks that make people comfortable. Occasionally, when some shrewd person would notice that I hadn't taken much, they'd pile more food on my plate or ask ever so carefully if I had eaten already because there was so little on my plate. I talked about having a big lunch or saving room for dessert or whatever else. Sometimes I did go back for seconds. People really don't notice when you eat more fruit than anything else; they don't see that you pile on the zero-calorie foods that will fill up a plate quick. And even if they do, the narratives that position the curviness of Black girls' bodies as a warning sign of future obesity will lead them to congratulating you on watching your weight instead of grasping that there is a problem playing out in full view. We are a culture that will accept eating disorders in plain sight; we'll call them clean eating or some other cute fad name, or we'll just plain pretend a disordered relationship with food is normal, as long as the person with it looks the way we expect. Our mental health is rarely anyone else's priority, courtesy of harmful myths about the strength of Black women.

Stress still makes me break up with food. It's easier now because I've put on enough weight that a skipped meal doesn't make anyone blink. And I have it largely under control, at least in the sense that I manage to eat twice a day even when food feels like a chore and not a joy. And I know that really means I still have an eating disorder. It's a thing I talk about in therapy with a lovely doctor who is content with my self-imposed rule. I'm not entirely certain she has a better plan for me. Black girls don't have eating disorders, you see, except when they do. There are a lot of things Black girls don't have. Safety, security, the kind of magic that erases colorism and racism and a dozen other -*isms*. We develop coping skills major and minor in the absence of better options. Sometimes those coping skills are good ones, like a daily walk or yoga; sometimes they are deeply unhealthy, whether that be disordered eating or some form of addiction.

Girls in marginalized communities have all of the same mental and emotional health issues as girls in wealthier communities (well, except affluenza, which is less a mental health condition in my opinion and more a convenient way to excuse horrible behavior), but they are less likely to have the resources or the language to address them. Yet they experience significant amounts of trauma and the attendant consequences.

Eating disorders are not really about eating habits, even though that is the most obvious symptom of the problem. In fact, eating disorders are rarely even about food. They are more likely to be about other issues in the home or around it. Whether it is divorce, poverty, abuse, or a mix of all of the above, an ED is the outward expression of other issues. They're also depressingly easy to hide in plain sight until the problem reaches a critical mass of ill health and blatant physical signs.

Not only do we reward thinness in general, we specifically reward any beauty aesthetic that prioritizes assimilation. For young people of color who are developing bodies that can never actually assimilate into the mythical monochrome of middle America, there's very little validation available in media or anywhere else.

Add in the deluge of imagery that associates beauty with whiteness, and for girls of color who are already struggling to love themselves in a world that tells them they are worth less than white girls, there is greater-than-average risk not only of them developing an eating disorder but also of it going unrecognized and untreated. And for the lucky few who do receive treatment, whether their program will address the impact of racism or be a source of yet more trauma is difficult to predict.

Although we're conditioned to think that most eating disorders develop at the onset of puberty, the truth is the seeds for them are laid much earlier. Children of color enter into prepubescent life with the painful awareness that no matter how many changes our bodies are going through, there's nothing about puberty that can meet standards set by white-centric, unreasonable

standards of beauty. Nor is there any part of adolescent development that can counter the anti-Blackness, the stereotypes, the
hypersexualization, and other issues facing marginalized communities. Puberty might be a primary trigger for people who
aren't from otherwise marginalized communities, but for people
of color, disabled people, nonbinary, and trans people, eating disorders are rooted in part in the structural factors that have been
impacting their view of themselves for most if not all of their
lives. We understand, for instance, that colorism impacts children as early as infancy, with people positioning the "prettiness"
of babies based on hair texture and eye color as a reason that
they want mixed-race children.

When we characterize eating disorders as the province of
well-off white girls, we ignore the impact of daily prejudice,
the many ways that having no safe spaces might make young
people of color feel powerless. Add in the constraints imposed
by the wealth gap, which impacts not only access to essential
things like a home, transportation, and safety but also the kinds
of extracurriculars that validate their cultural context and self-
image, and there is a recipe for disaster. When you control nothing in your environment and are constantly bombarded with
media messages that tell you that your body is simply wrong, it
can make you feel that your body is the only thing you can control. Unfortunately, these kinds of socioeconomic variables go ignored by health-care providers because of institutional bias.

You don't develop healthy eating habits when food is yet another battle against racism or poverty or both. You can't have a

healthy relationship with your body when your body is treated as criminal simply for existing.

And when we bring in the kinds of foods that are held up as healthy, cultural differences can leave marginalized people feeling alienated. Pretty pictures on Instagram, on food blogs, and in magazines of the latest healthier diets and meal plans valorized as quick fixes can increase anxiety. The messaging is inescapable; even if you don't look at the magazines that are in every waiting room, there are the ads on Facebook, there are commercials on TV, there's a never-ending stream of celebrity meal plans being discussed. Not only are the bodies in those images overwhelmingly slim, white, abled, and cis, the food isn't necessarily appealing or familiar. Someone living in a food desert wouldn't even be able to afford the ingredients the articles tout, and even for someone who might be able to get most of the ingredients, the flavor profiles might not be palatable. For that matter, after decades of ethnic cuisines being blamed for poor health outcomes, the reality is that many of these "elevated" recipes are blander and more expensive versions packaged in ways that are offensive.

Eating healthier is hard if the options available within your budget aren't like anything you might experience in your community. It stays in the magazines or the cutesy Facebook videos and doesn't look or feel like real life because it is so distant and unattainable that it might as well be elf bread. It becomes easier to not eat or to fall into a cycle of bingeing and purging than to try to figure out how to attain this unattainable body in any way that might be healthy. Meanwhile even though we know that body mass index isn't really useful or healthy, and we are increasingly aware that diets don't work, we still as a society hold up thin white bodies as the standard of healthy. You might expect the medical industry to be better than to feed into a disordered relationship with food. But doctors are more likely to ignore all available research that shows that being overweight doesn't increase mortality in favor of their own fatphobia.

Even organizations that exist to address eating disorders are working from a lack of data due to the medical community's assumption that eating disorders largely affect white women. There's relatively little research that is inclusive enough to address racial differences, much less gender or disability issues. Although there's a growing awareness that eating disorders span all communities, even professional organizations related to the treatment of eating disorders can lack cultural competence in how they discuss not only the incidence rate but also causes.

Primary texts still in use largely ignore the impact of socioeconomic status and identity on relationships with food. *The Eating Disorder Sourcebook: A Comprehensive Guide to the Causes, Treatments, and Prevention of Eating Disorders* by Carolyn Costin addresses issues of ethnicity and gender in just eight of its pages despite being in its third edition. *Eating Disorders: A Reference Sourcebook* by Raymond Lemberg and Leigh Cohn, first published in 1999, does address eating disorders in men, but doesn't talk about race, nonbinary or trans issues, or disability. This absence of information is perversely harmful because it not only erases individuality, it further isolates those struggling with disordered eating. Instead of addressing them as individuals with complex lives affected by family dynamics, economics, and popular culture, it makes them ghosts in a machine that grinds them down as fodder for an industry that ultimately harms everyone including the thin white women who are supposed to be aspirational examples. It's a systemic bias that quickly crumbles in the face of lived experience. Every community has its own standards, but those are harder to hear over the roar of the mainstream.

When we talk about bodies and how they engage with the world and how the world engages with them, we have to ask ourselves why we love the trappings of so many cultures on white bodies but not on the bodies of those who created these looks.

When media criticizes Ciara's faux locs and then calls the same hairstyle edgy on a Kardashian, what message is being sent to young girls of color? If bandannas are a hot new accessory for young white women in the pages of *Elle* and a reason to throw handcuffs on a Latina in high school, then what message is received? What impact does it have to pretend that cornrows on white women are the same as a weave on Black women when only one is likely to lose their job over a hairstyle? We know colorism exists, but do we grasp the ways that the message that lighter skin is better are reinforced before we criticize bleaching?

It's important to remember that this is all happening within a society that privileges lighter skin over darker skin, that prioritizes able bodies over disabled bodies, that sees being cisgender as the only option. Although not everyone will develop mental illnesses around their body image as a result of this environment, for those who do, the illness is often reinforced because it can appear to be a way to gain social status. For a marginalized person, fitting into a specific aesthetic can have benefits such as higher-paying jobs, better access to education, and better treatment by society at large. It isn't just about being considered more attractive; for many, it could be the determinant of access to quality housing, or even how they are treated by the legal system.

We have to understand that every "It's just hair," "It's just a Halloween costume," "It's just makeup" defense given for white bodies to be validated at the expense of those of color is another weight on the scales pushing mental health issues into marginalized communities. The trauma experienced may be lower in levels, but it can also be a constant stressor with no way to escape short of retreating from the larger world entirely.

The truth is no one is immune to trauma, but only some get what they need to handle the aftermath. Overwhelmingly mental health resources are hard to access regardless of the issue. As a result, far too often people who are experiencing trauma find coping mechanisms that just displace the pain instead of addressing it.

There's the potential stigma attached to the idea of needing mental health treatment or cultural expectations that someone in pain seek help from religion rather than psychology or psychiatry. For those who grow up in the church, prayer is more likely to be recommended than Prozac. And while there's nothing wrong with finding prayer comforting, it can't fix brain chemistry. A pastor might be able to provide counsel in the moment at a hospital or after a loss, but they are unlikely to be able to offer regular weekly sessions like a trained therapist.

There's also the problem of finding culturally competent providers in a mental health system that is weighted heavily toward Eurocentric values and cultural norms. Having to combat racism, bias, and discrimination outside and then deal with it in treatment can drive those most in need away from resources. And of course in America, there are always the problems caused by a lack of adequate health insurance coverage.

We know from recent research that PTSD is a serious problem for inner-city youth across the United States. When situated in the context of geographic racial segregation, this also means that PTSD among youth is overwhelmingly a problem for youth of color. There's some evidence that PTSD can be a trigger for eating disorders. Does that mean that the two are always linked? Of course not, but what could we see if we considered the mental health of people in underserved communities the same way that we focus on the mental and emotional health of middle-class white people?

Unhealthy coping mechanisms can range from disordered eating to cutting to addiction. When we talk about marginalized youth in mainstream feminist circles, we tend to focus on narratives that ignore how much of success is reliant on one having the internal resources to persevere. It's less about respectability narratives and more about empowering emotional health initiatives. Overeating and refusing to eat are unhealthy, but they are also common responses to anxiety and stress. What can be more stressful than living in communities that feel like they are under siege? How do you cope when your anxiety starts out as a symptom of unrecognized and untreated PTSD? I can't say whether my PTSD or my ED came first, but I know that when I was finally able to access therapy that specifically focused on treating trauma, I experienced a reduction in all of my symptoms.

The myths of the Strong Black Woman from chapter one, the Wise Indian, the Submissive Asian, and the Sassy Latina do more than show up in bad TV shows. They influence the perception that women who are not white do not experience a full range of emotions, much less suffer from the same mental health issues. It doesn't help that marginalized youths can be inundated with hateful messages—in classroom material and on social media—that undermine any sense of safety and security in ways that are not always readily apparent to people who do not experience the same kinds of oppression. Color blindness doesn't always work in casting, and it certainly doesn't work in community health initiatives that should be intrinsically feminist. After all, if we want to preach body positivity and equality, then we have to be mindful not only of the bodies that we celebrate but also of the struggles that those bodies may have faced.

White supremacy comes in many disguises, but the way it moves through spaces that claim to be body positive is perhaps one of the most insidious. The only way to challenge it is to pause and think critically and honestly about impact. That doesn't mean you should never appreciate a culture or participate in it, but you should be willing to interrogate the social and cultural context. While Rachel Dolezal is one of the more extreme examples,

as she has essentially been appropriating an entire racial identity in service of a greater crime, the sad reality is that she likely
started out with these claims as a way of making herself feel better without any concern for impact.

We have to consider that representation matters not just on
screens or in books but also in the community. Bigotry impacts
the mental health of marginalized people, as well as the social
and economic health. When your body is treated as fundamentally less human, when your emotional range is presented as too
stunted to appreciate how you've been dehumanized by a movement that claims to be for you, then where do you turn to start
healing? Sometimes the most feminist thing to do is to consider
the idea that what makes you feel pretty, what makes you think
of yourself as sexy, isn't happening in a vacuum. It has real consequences for communities that you don't inhabit, and it's not
excusable just because it makes the person appropriating feel
attractive.

Although body-positive feminism is supposed to celebrate
everyone, there are recurring issues of racism and colorism even
within that community. Because white female bodies being adored
and protected is a key aspect of maintaining white supremacist narratives, there is a side effect of alienating the very communities of color that started the body-positive movement. When
white feminism takes the center of any conversation about bodies, there is a tendency to replicate the same harmful aesthetics
that prioritize certain body types to uphold as worthwhile and
prioritize others as worth ignoring or outright shaming. Unsur-
prisingly there's a lack of concern for the mental health of those

being pushed out of a movement that was supposed to be inclusive.

It's important to understand that stress and trauma extend beyond the direct behaviors of prejudiced individuals and impact communities. When people are surrounded by constant reminders that their identity is unwelcome, and microaggressions can come at anytime, anywhere, to anyone, it creates a lingering anxiety around your body's right to exist. It may seem like I am commingling disparate issues within the community, but for marginalized people, the messaging that our bodies are wrong and a problem to be solved by disappearing can feel constant.

We regularly see clips on the news featuring unarmed Black, Latinx, Asian, or Indigenous people being killed on the street, in a car, in a holding cell, or even in a church. Not only does that bring up an array of painful memories, it can trigger something called vicarious traumatization. Even if the specific event has never happened to us directly, we may have witnessed similar experiences, or know people in our communities who have been traumatized or killed in similar ways. Not only are their stories resonating in our minds, there's never a shortage of pundits getting airtime to justify the horror that has occurred. Victim blaming isn't just something that occurs around sexual assault, and because the cycle of trauma never ends, you expect to be able to embrace the idea of self-care as a way to cope. To be able to rest your mind in the spaces that ostensibly exist online and off for that purpose. So it can be incredibly jarring to seek out safer spaces and find that you aren't necessarily welcome or cared for in the same way because of your identity.

Marginalized people are more likely to have lower levels of access to mental health services than middle- or upper-class white people, and when they receive care, it is more likely to be of poorer quality. There are several factors that create situations where marginalized people in high-stress environments aren't getting proper care. In some areas like Chicago, it can be as simple as a lack of availability due to closures of mental health programs. Even for those who still have programs available, other barriers to care may include transportation issues, a lack of childcare, or difficulty taking time off work to attend regular appointments.

We know that the mental health system is flawed, but that's not a good excuse for feminism to ignore the emotional health of women of color. Instead of parroting dehumanizing racist tropes about the strength of marginalized people, feminism has to be willing to interrogate its stake in upholding this aspect of white supremacy. Advocates for medical care should also be working on improving the status quo for those who are the least likely to both seek and receive treatment. Feminism has to center on those who are most vulnerable to the systemic disparities in conversations around getting help and caring for yourself, whether through the mental health system or at home. It's not enough to do a token highlight of the problems in marginalized communities once a year. Feminism has to advocate for better access to mental health care for everyone.

It's also important to not off-load the emotional labor of educating providers or communities onto the marginalized people looking for support. And it's key to include marginalized people in leadership roles in campaigns and in institutions that claim to be concerned with mental health. Above all, it's essential to do the work of lobbying legislators at all levels to improve access to quality mental health services in every area. We can't afford to keep pretending that mental health issues stop at the boundaries of whiteness. Instead we have to be ready, willing, and able to embrace those for whom mental health is a struggle and to make sure that we aren't contributing to their trauma under the guise of being helpful.

THE FETISHIZATION
OF FIERCE

Depending on who you ask, I am either fiercely feminist or incredibly toxic. There's something about being willing to step into open conflict with anyone who tries you that can upset people, can confuse them. It doesn't help that my particular approach to conflict can be scathing. But for the people who are more likely to describe me as fierce than as toxic, they enjoy the knowledge that I have no problem speaking up. That I am always completely and totally willing to fight back. There seems to be a very thin line between fierce and toxic in feminist circles these days (I have been called both at various points, and honestly neither ever seemed to quite fit), but one of the things I have noticed about the term *fierce* is that it carries its own highly specialized baggage.

The women most likely to be called fierce are also those most likely to be facing the greatest social risks. The same tired tropes always end up being trotted out. The Angry Black Woman, the

Sassy Latina, and so on. What we ignore is that those narratives inform how we view the women we claim to venerate. We think of Beyoncé's feminism as fierce right up until she turns out to be a human being who loves her spouse more than the idea of the Strong Independent Woman Who Doesn't Need a Man.

We adore Serena Williams until she's visibly angry while challenging a system that continually harasses her with drug tests and questionable calls from line judges. Then we think she's too angry and needs to calm down. They're warriors, but apparently not the right kind of warriors. Serena is castigated for her facial expressions during games, after games, when she talks about the sport at all, for responding to the sexism of referees, even for not being a good role model because she's not polite enough in her responses to sexism and racism in her sport.

Yet their careers and their lives are amazing examples of the power to succeed as women in male-dominated industries. There's something so wonderful about having the power to come from working-class roots to acquire not just fame and fortune, but the power to shape the culture. They give young Black women the power to delight in beauty and sexuality by having the kinds of careers that dominate mainstream media while still championing feminism as a powerful force for the good of girls. Yet when they have the audacity to not only claim feminism, but feel like they get to dictate and direct the way that they engage with it, there's some sense that suddenly they are less qualified because they used their bodies—much maligned, much analyzed bodies—to achieve those careers.

Critics still question their idea of female empowerment. They want them to wear more clothes, to not be so strong or so sexy, or to not be so cheerfully, enthusiastically unconcerned with hitting a checklist of "appropriate" feminist milestones. But fiercely fighting your way past the boundaries that white supremacy might set isn't for the faint of heart. We know, after all, that well-behaved women don't make history. Still, as the criticism of both Beyoncé and Serena ramped up, as the backlash for them choosing to go their own way spread out to criticism not just of their careers, but of their personal lives, even of their children, it was clear that being so fierce had consequences.

And while those two women have the resources and the networks required to insulate themselves, the average woman fighting against the patriarchy is more likely to be far less privileged. Yet the demands that the risks be taken by those without the insulation of racial privilege never abate. Instead the narrative is one that lauds the courage of those who do take the risks, with very little discussion of the possible aftermath. Whether it is being outspoken about police brutality, harassment, and sexual assault in politics, entertainment, tech, or other industries, too often those who speak out are positioned more as sacrifices than saviors. When the seemingly inevitable backlash complete with harassment and death threats starts, some feminists will speak up; many will simply suggest contacting the police or the FBI, but they won't offer anything else. And if anyone brings up the lack of meaningful support for victims, the conversation is quickly shifted to center on those who didn't take the risk.

In my experience, when I have been targeted or other Black women have been the primary targets of harassment, Black women have had to back each other up on social media. This is especially true on platforms like Twitter, where filtering out trolls is made more difficult by the lack of quality tools to handle the deluge of voices. When Jamilah Lemieux, then an editor at *Ebony*, was targeted by conservative trolls, it was Black feminist Twitter that backed her up. Whether the reason for the harassment is being pro-choice, a critique of the political choices of a GOP spokesperson, or something like what has happened to professors like Anthea Butler, Eve Ewing, and other Black academics, they are at best lauded for their fierceness from a distance by white feminist writers. More often they are ignored, or as has been the case with House representative Ilhan Omar, they are targets of white feminists like Chelsea Clinton, until the rhetoric spills over into actual physical violence.

Suddenly the same women who adore fierceness, who celebrate ideals like speaking truth to power, are all about their own personal fragility. After all, being fierce has its consequences. And besides, it's not like they're the police. They aren't responsible for protecting anyone, for helping anyone access safety, or for connecting anyone with resources. Well, not anyone inconvenient, anyway. Not when there was a carceral solution that they could rely on at their fingertips.

We know that carceral feminism (a reliance on policing, prosecution, and imprisonment to resolve gendered or sexual violence) is most likely to be used against women who fight back. Particularly women of color. The state responds to public concerns around sexual violence by re-traumatizing victims. It rarely offers them anything approaching justice. The carceral impulse also informs how feminism responds to victims before, during, and after they attempt to press charges or otherwise combat the patriarchy. What has arisen repeatedly in feminism is a tendency to assume that once victims have gone to the state, their needs are all met. This is especially obvious in the responses to online harassment.

While many feminists have no problem arguing for criminalizing the behavior, they are light on ways to safeguard those experiencing it. Because of the impact of a carceral approach, we see a framework that restricts feminist horizons to structures that expect the individual to fight rather than the collective. This form of individualist feminism relies on the idea that an empowered woman can do anything. It ignores the economic and racial realities that some face.

What does individualist feminism look like in practice? While we stand on the sidelines cheering women on, largely there has been minimal collective efforts to fight oppression across multiple identities. We ignore the fact that the same structures affect us all (albeit differently), and we rely on the myths of strength rather than on any understanding of what it means to work together.

It doesn't help that when welfare reform was enacted, politicians ignored the fact that victims of domestic violence, sexual assault, and so on might not be able to go back to work immediately or at all. Without funding for public housing and other social safety nets, low-income survivors in particular found themselves "helped" right out of any measure of stability.

While we laud the strength of those who fight back, this

sometimes leads to victims being arrested for defending them-selves. This is especially true in the case of sex workers, victims of domestic violence, and others who find themselves squeezed by the system that prioritizes imprisoning them over protect-ing them. The same carceral solutions that imprison them have taken the place of the infrastructure that allowed survivors some measure of freedom to live independently without having to rely on abusers. After all, if you can access affordable housing and welfare programs, your options are already broader than if you cannot.

It's not that the actions of survivors to defend themselves are necessarily bad or wrong. The state gives them very few op-tions to prevent violence, and many ways to report the after-math. For those who are not lucky enough to attract broader media attention, self-defense might open the door for them to lose years of their life to imprisonment. But when we only have carceral solutions to social problems, there is very little room for actual justice, much less healing.

In feminist circles the "fierce" warrior narrative is often held up as an honor given to the women who take the biggest risks in their careers or otherwise. "Oh, she's so brave to press charges." "It takes a strong woman to do what she did." It sounds great in passing, the idea of those who fought the patriarchy being stron-ger, braver, more ferocious than those who did not take the same risks. But what we don't talk about is what that costs victims. While they are fighting their way through whatever obstacles and feminism stands on the sidelines cheering them on, what happens when the coolness fades? Do we have a safety net, an idea of how to provide for the potential financial and social consequences?

Too often those who take the risks have very little in the way of a backup plan and are staring down the barrel of a life after activism with the same poverty and lack of social and emotional resources, and even more obstacles because of infamy and in some situations a criminal record. For everyone who might win a high-dollar settlement (money can't buy happiness, but it can buy some measure of stability), thousands more must figure out how to navigate life after losing. Some of our biggest icons die in relative obscurity, impoverished and alone, dependent on the kindness of strangers or the cold, clinical mercies of the state.

We love the idea of a Strong Black Woman, celebrate those who, like Anita Hill, manage to continue to have a successful career in the aftermath. But what about those who can't do that? For those without a pass back to middle class or the ivory tower, what resources are available? The same feminism that holds them up to fight the battles turns away when the war is over and doesn't bother to tend the wounds, emotional or otherwise.

Being strong or fierce or whatever appellation is applied to the ones who get brutalized, who sue, who wind up in the ground with those she leaves behind begging the world to #SayHerName sounds great, but the labels are cold comfort if we don't do more to solve the problems that they are fighting. For organizers and activists these frameworks are sometimes already in place, but for the average feminist trying to fight a local social ill, especially those living in low-income communities, society as a whole has failed to provide adequate resources. Equality is great, but equity is better precisely because the emotional validation someone with financial security and the insulation of privilege might need is nearly useless for someone without those things. It's the Strong Black Woman problem writ large enough to include other communities, though still most likely to impact Black and Brown women.

We expect marginalized voices to ring out no matter what obstacles they face, and then we penalize them for not saying the right thing in the right way. We assign a level of resilience that is unparalleled and then once it is met, we assume that the person displaying it doesn't have feelings. Or more accurately, we decide that they don't need anyone to care about their feelings. In fact, mainstream feminism renders the feelings of white women as the primary concern, even in situations that are emphatically not about them. Take Jill Biden's announcement in support of her husband's campaign that it is time for people to move on from discussing his treatment of Anita Hill despite the clear evidence that he has his own legacy of inappropriate and unwanted contact with women. Or Alyssa Milano's response to the Georgia abortion ban with an abstinence-based "solution" that ignores the reality that those most likely to be negatively impacted are the Black and Brown women in Georgia who aren't part-time residents.

This is the dirty underbelly of the perceived fierceness of Black and Brown women. Ultimately, the fierceness narrative is a millstone around the neck, dragging them down and endangering their chances at survival. Because pop culture and media teach us that low-income women exist to serve, to be the work-horses, we don't consider what they may need.

We frame them as cold, undereducated, sassy, emotional, and actual servants to advance the cause of feminism. Quietly inserted into the narratives of their lives are idealized Mammy and Nanny expectations. Girls from the hood don't need help because they can protect themselves against everything, or so mainstream feminism believes. They are ready to brawl, to be hood rats and harridans who can force the world to change, but who clearly lack answers for the problems they face inside their communities. They are simultaneously the first responders and the last to get resources. The same fear of the hood that prevents mainstream feminism from entering it without gentrifying it also contributes to the idea that no one needs to care about the scary angry women who live there, unless they can be useful.

We must move away from the strategies provided by corporate feminism that teach us to lean in but not how to actually support each other. Organizations and initiatives are wonderful ways to tackle certain societal ills, but overwhelmingly they do little to provide care or access to care for those who need it. A victim-centered approach is more than just a phrase that looks good on paper; it has to be a key component of how we structure responses to those who fought to advance the causes that feminism holds dear. We don't even need to create a diagram in order to accomplish this goal; it already exists. We can look at existing victim-advocacy programs, can structure our responses both virtual and otherwise, to insulate victims.

In a victim-centered approach, the victim's wishes, safety, and well-being take priority. Victim-centered feminism would bring to bear specialized services, resources, cultural competence, and, ideally, trauma-informed perspectives toward caring for the needs of those who go through the trauma of testifying or pressing charges or filing lawsuits. We would provide a conduit to the professionals best able to assess survivor needs, and we'd provide critical support to survivors in the aftermath even if they were not eligible for traditional victim-support services that may exist in their area. These skills are imperative to building rapport and trust with survivors, meeting their needs, and assisting them in creating a sense of safety and security in their lives.

We need to be tackling the loss of critical community resources ranging from mental health-care clinics to housing. We need to understand that sometimes the fiercest warriors need care and kindness. We can't be afraid of their anger or their willingness to shout. We love that fierce energy in the moment, but we need to embrace it across time. We need to shift our ideas of who deserves support and move away from the idea that after the case everything is fixed.

THE HOOD DOESN'T HATE SMART PEOPLE

I have what my mother calls euphemistically a rebellious spirit. It's a nice way to describe a child who is not what you expected. This does not mean that I was always strong, always sure, or anything even remotely close to the narratives of inborn self-confidence often foisted on young Black bodies to excuse the premature expectations of adulthood. I was a cowardly child who (a) hated fighting—literally cried through a fight because I hated fighting; and (b) threw my whole self into the fight anyway. I wasn't a good fighter. I was just a child who understood that not wanting to fight is meaningless sometimes. There is a lot of research around young women of color and fighting, a narrative that lends itself to the idea that they are violent for the sake of violence. It ignores the fact that they are often the only people with an investment in their own safety outside their nearest and dearest.

I wasn't a cool kid. I was a nerd; my nickname was Books.

And yes, I got teased for talking so proper and reading so much. But it wasn't the "Black people don't value education" trope that gets trotted out so often. There were lots of smart kids at my grammar school, Charles S. Kozminski. We were all poor, so there was relatively little difference in our clothes in terms of price. Style was the key, and I had none. *None.* I was two years younger than everyone else in my grade, and my grandmother's sense of style was age appropriate but not grade appropriate. She bought me the kind of clothes you dress little girls in that are prissy images of girlhood. Lace tights, Mary Janes, and full skirts, while everyone else was in overalls and gym shoes. I stuck out and not in a good way. It didn't help that I sounded like I was reading from a dictionary half the time. Fortunately, I had friends who understood the social perils of being raised by a grandparent; they nudged me to hang out, to talk like the other kids did when the adults weren't listening. I learned to code-switch sometime between seventh grade and twelfth grade. But I was always a nerd.

There's a trend in some of these feminist books to tell you that the hood punishes you for being smart, that it hates those who reach for success. That wasn't my experience at all. The same kids who called me Books are now adults who pass my articles around and tell me how proud of me they are, because there was nothing malicious in the teasing. I teased, I was teased; that's basically the nature of kids. There's a myth of exceptionalism attached to people who succeed academically after a childhood in poverty. We must be unique and thus worth listening to, but at the price of leaving behind the past and the people in it. You're supposed to look back on those years as though they were this hardscrabble time and you would never expose your child to the same things—if you even have a child, because after all, growing up there is scarring, the kind of thing that might mean you have to sacrifice everything else to claw your way out.

It's a comforting idea to some that aspiring to a place at the table comes at a cost, that success for marginalized people means leaving behind their culture and community because it isn't good enough to get them where they want to go. But that's a myth that opens the door for some women to be shut out of conversations that directly affect them. Being "one of those people" lends itself to a unique and useful ability to understand not only how something can be helpful but also how it can be twisted to hurt the people it is meant to serve.

Class and classism matter here; this isn't something that springs up out of nowhere. We treat being poor, being from the inner city, being from the country as reasons to be ashamed even though no one controls the circumstances of their own birth. We look at places that are being starved of resources, where being tough is a matter of survival, and then we say, "In order to have safety, financial stability, housing that isn't subpar, you have to be willing to cut away everything that made you," and when some people can't or won't do that we punish them for it. It's assimilation, not acculturation, that is demanded of people who are already sacrificing, already making hard choices. Yet whenever a problem arises, those same skills are what everyone needs to make it. Ask your elders about bread lines and soup kitchens; ask them about who steps in immediately after a disaster, natural or otherwise. Invariably it is those with the least who are the most generous. It is women who are worried about their own homes and families who comfort themselves by cooking pots of soup to feed rescuers. It is men who have nothing to lose who climb into the wreckage without masks or gloves to pull out those who had everything and lost it. The things are replaceable, the people are not, is the logic. Unfortunately, that kind of compassion isn't as common in reverse.

I'm a descendant of enslaved people. My great-great-great-grandmother Mary Gamble was sold on Sullivan's Island, and that is as much as I will ever know about her origins. It was theorized that she wasn't completely African based on her reported complexion, but there's no way to know. We know more about her children—my great-great-grandfather AB, or Abraham, was gifted to one of his white half-siblings when the family decided to move from South Carolina to Arkansas. His children were born into slavery, though they were freed after the Civil War. My great-grandfather's land is still technically in the family, though my grandfather never lived on it after childhood. He had a temper, you see, and so he went north, because otherwise he was going to get himself or someone else killed. That was the fear, anyway, and he was a hard man, so perhaps this was a valid concern. By the time I met him, he was on the usher board at Blackwell AME Zion, but people told stories about a man who tried to rob him, and the way he dumped that man in the ambulance bay at County.

He met my grandmother in Chicago. She was the granddaughter of enslaved people. We don't know as much about her family history; a lot of it was a secret, though I do know that her mother, Penny Rose, was the first woman in my maternal line to legally be able to read. I've gotten far enough back in the research to know that her mother was enslaved for a time in Georgia and her father was enslaved in Louisiana, but I have no idea how they met or a host of other details. There was a lynching, you see, some murder (my family believes in revenge in ways that I can't quite explain), and then they moved. They left the South, came to Chicago, Detroit, spread west to California. Penny Rose ran a policy wheel and I was raised by Dorothy, who was also involved in policy. Vice and sacrifice paved the way.

Survival can be a religion unto itself, and for many it's the only one that they always have time to practice. Putting food on the table, giving the next generation a better shot at success by way of relocation or education. The hood doesn't lack answers; it lacks resources, and so the priorities beyond basic survival are how to accumulate enough to set the next generation up for more success.

I have a bachelor's from the University of Illinois at Urbana-Champaign and a master's from DePaul in Chicago. My great-aunts were educated, though my grandmother left college during the war, and there's a weird story about her working for the US Army Signal Corps that might in fact be a cover for her working in cryptanalysis. Dorothy loved her puzzles and her mysteries and her codes, and she was frankly a genius who never got the credit she probably deserved. But she raised strong, smart children. Complicated children, but still, she made sure that we knew what price was paid to get us here.

I tried to drop out of high school once, and by tried, I mean I mentioned taking the GED because I was a sixteen-year-old senior having a miserable time in school. I was bored and restless, and I told my grandmother my grand plan. She had just had a radical mastectomy and I was hanging out with her because, well, elders really matter in my community. You listen to them, you spend time with them, and I talked to my grandmother every day about everything. We had a great relationship that was only in peril for the approximately thirty seconds when I thought dropping out to get my GED was a good idea. Pro tip: Never tell a woman who lived through Jim Crow, who grew up with grandparents who had been enslaved, who had a mother who'd worked tirelessly to make things better for her kids, that you want to throw away your chance at a diploma. I mean, you could, but I promise you, you are not built for the moment you get snatched up by a hand that is harder than steel while she informs you about what your ancestors paid in blood to buy your access to education.

Education wasn't the only thing on the table. I grew up with the arts because one of my great-aunts wanted to be an actress; another aunt sang in church. Some of you will recognize by now the kind of family I had: they were never well-off, though they were often comfortable enough to afford wants. Still it was life in an apartment and sharing a room, but there were trips to the library and getting my hair done at Josephine's on Forty-ninth and a school that was poor but excellent. Middle-class aspirations in a working-class family that knew that respectability hadn't brought them a thing, but that hard work can happen in a lot of ways.

I never thought there was only one way to be Black or that Black Americans were less-than, though I went through periods of deep fascination with roots. I am still interested in roots, but I know now that the seeds of my family were from across the water, and my roots are here in America. My kids are sixth-generation and possibly seventh (the details of whether my maternal great grandparents, Mariah and Andrew, were born here are fuzzy, but Penny Rose's stories to her children make it sound like they were), and there is no going backward. I will never know the cultures that birthed them or their ancestors. I can never lay claim to those cultures, because they are not mine, not even if I move into one of the countries that would pop up on a DNA test. That road is closed. That's okay; there is a way forward. We always go forward.

When I stand between people who would disrespect elders, who would demean or denigrate the grief of a community, I am not always nice. And kindness in my definition is not the one some others would use. But what I will never be ashamed of is the knowledge that Black American equals a unique and distinct cultural context that deserves respect, and the same careful approach as any other in the diaspora. There is an idea created by white supremacy and fostered by anti-Blackness that Black Americans have no culture to own or defend, that anyone can move into our culture and communities, stand outside the context, and declare themselves a part of what was built through sacrifice and suffering. It is the commodification of Black cool on white bodies, it is the narrative that Black Americans are lazy, it is the erroneous conflation of Black American hypervisibility with power and privilege. And while I firmly believe anyone in the diaspora is welcome to tread paths we carved out, and to carve out their own, I will never back down from protecting the legacy of those who paved the way for me and my children.

Too often the legacy of slavery crops up in the assumption that Black Americans are not taking advantage of opportunity, with no understanding of the impact of generational racism and anti-Blackness on our communities. It's easy to assume that we all come to the table from places that are healthy, but realistically that isn't possible, not when we remember that while flowers can bloom in the harshest environments, many plants simply die. I was lucky—I had someone to take me in, to raise me and feed me, and catch me when I might have slipped. I am obligated not only to give back, but to challenge erasure and disrespect where I find it, because the children I am raising and the children who are being raised need to see that they are the inheritors of a proud enduring legacy forged here by the people who were put into chains and the people who broke them.

Whether we're talking about the hood, the rez, or the barrio, the truth is that no community hates learning or success. Nerds come from all walks of life, but accessing the lifestyle that those things are supposed to provide is much more difficult than it should be for marginalized people.

It's no surprise that a narrative of "being smart is acting white, so other marginalized people hate you" resonates with a lot of people. After all, it echoes a narrow, stereotypical image of what it means to be Black, to be Latinx, Asian, or Indigenous. It validates the prejudices of adults who remember feeling that they were different, and remember conflating that feeling with ostracism. It's an easy explanation for being smart but not popular in school; that doesn't require thinking about the reality that children, like adults, react to more than the surface. It ignores the adults who might have rewarded academically successful children at the expense of children who struggled. And for those who are only vaguely interested in improving educational outcomes, it promises a quick fix by way of attitude adjustment instead of actual investment.

It's a theory that not only appeals to those who want to retroactively feel special and unique but also validates conservative ideology by placing the blame for disparate academic outcomes squarely on the backs of children. By making the lack of opportunity about cultural pathology instead of broader factors like inequality, racial bias, and segregation, survivors can cozy up to whiteness and absolve themselves of any meaningful responsibility to the community. Feeling isolated in sixth grade is common, but only some communities are assigned a narrative that makes it about being too smart, and not about more mundane things like clothes, hygiene, or social awkwardness.

I know that everyone's road to acceptance and embrace of their culture is not the same, and that a collective understanding of what it means to succeed at all costs is ultimately impossible. But as we talk about feminism and Black Girl Magic and the folks who make a way out of no way, we need to welcome the idea that those who pushed us ahead weren't valuable just because of what that did for us as individuals. They have and had value in their own right. The shadow economies they build are about survival and success, but they are also about making sure that no matter what happens, the future is always an option. White savior narratives embedded in feminist rhetoric tend to position the people who don't get out as not being worth the effort of engagement, of needing to be led toward progressive ideologies instead of understanding that the conversations that need to happen between the proverbial hood and the hills are ones between equals who have had to face different obstacles to arrive at the same destination.

MISSING AND MURDERED

I've technically gone missing several times in my life. When I was eight, it was falling asleep at a friend's house during recess. When I was sixteen, it was getting in the car with an ex I thought I could trust and drinking something that knocked me out for over a hundred miles. The first time, my teacher noticed that my friend and I were missing. The second time, no one noticed, but I came away from the experience wiser, if not unscathed. I might have gone missing a third time in my early twenties while walking in Mainz, Germany.

But by then, I was no longer in the business of ignoring my instincts. Not in the tiny dark tunnel under the bridge between Mainz and Mainz-Kastel. Not in the middle of the night when a man blocked the exit with his car and demanded I join him for a party. My German was terrible, but it was enough for me to understand that it wasn't a party I wanted to attend. I ran at him, ran across the hood of his car, and perhaps my foot grazed his face on my way to safety. I wasn't sure if I was in any real danger in the tunnel under the bridge, but I didn't want to find out. Fortunately, it turned out that a lot of luck, street smarts, and a well-placed kick can save you sometimes. I was scared, lectured by a Turkish grandmother, but I got to go back to my apartment that night.

I can't say I never had another scare like that; I'm a Chicago girl, and for a number of reasons, it is easy to be Black and go missing here. Almost as easy as it is to be Indigenous and go missing, or to be a Latinx and go missing, to be trans and of color and go missing. Sometimes that means that someone has been murdered and no one knows what happened, because the trail was cold from the start. As a result of Missing White Woman Syndrome, a phenomenon where media coverage of white women who have gone missing blankets the airwaves (sometimes off and on for decades), it's no surprise that when women disappear from marginalized communities, the issue doesn't always get a lot of attention. Excuses are made about drugs, risky behavior, or simply that the missing person in question is an adult who likely moved on to someone else somewhere else. Even when the bodies pile up, it is entirely possible that the police will ignore them because of their race.

Right now, in Chicago there are clusters of murdered Black and Brown women whose bodies have been found since 2001 and their murders are largely going unsolved. Chicago police have insisted there is no evidence of a serial killer in action, though in a city with a police murder clearance rate of only 25 percent it's difficult to assess how much work has been done to solve these crimes. Murder clearance rates are down around the country, with a national average of 59 percent, but Chicago's is among the lowest in the country. Even though the Chicago Police Department has admitted that there might be an active serial killer on the loose after two decades and more than fifty deaths, after so many years, what are the chances that these crimes can be solved? Potential witnesses have forgotten details, moved away, or even died.

According to the FBI's National Crime Information Center, despite being only 13 percent of the total population, Black Americans account for an average of 34 percent of all missing persons every year. Grassroots efforts ranging from websites like Black and Missing to candlelight vigils, flyers, and social media campaigns on Twitter and Facebook are important tools to generate attention, but they are no match for mainstream news coverage or better efforts by the government. Social media has also made it possible for families who can't get traditional media attention on their own to potentially go viral and end up with more people looking for their lost loved ones.

But at least there has been some effort by the government to keep track of missing Black people through collecting racially specific data, even if there is minimal follow-up to solve the cases. The categories used to track data largely rely on a Black-white binary approach to the American population and obscure other racial and ethnic identifiers. Only in the past ten years has there been any real effort by the FBI to track the numbers of missing Indigenous women. And while the Canadian government has invested resources in tracking what is happening there, the

United States lags far behind despite promises by the government to do better.

A study by the Urban Indian Health Institute showed that of the 5,712 cases of missing Indigenous women reported in 2016, only 116 were logged in the Department of Justice database. Data analysis also shows that some counties had murder rates of Indigenous women that were more than ten times the national average. Unfortunately, the quality of this data is limited by the willingness of individuals to report violence to police and of law enforcement to designate deaths as homicide. A 2014 study in the *American Journal of Public Health* on causes of death in Indigenous American communities using data collected between 1999 and 2009 found that Indigenous women have a homicide rate triple that of white women.

Similarly, Latinx face a lack of investment in their safety, especially under the auspices of a government led by white supremacist men and enabled by white supremacist women to pretend that they don't even deserve to seek safety. Buried in the anti-immigrant rhetoric that the GOP is currently espousing to justify building a wall is the sad fact that, as the United Nations High Commissioner for Refugees reports, many of the women from Central America seeking asylum are fleeing gender violence.

Women and children, especially girls, as well as LGBTQIA people continue to face high levels of gender-based violence in the United States and around the world. Femicide (the murder of women) is a global issue. For example, in El Salvador, ranked number one in the world in female homicide, there were a reported 469 femicides in 2017, which means that on average, more than nine women or girls were killed every week in 2017. Many of the Latinx asylum seekers are women, children, and LGBTQIA people fleeing brutal physical and sexual violence at the hands of gang members and other individuals at home. Unfortunately, they may not find much greater safety in the United States or in Canada. We know that in the United States, an average of three women are killed every day by someone they know, usually a current or former partner. But because of the high number of missing persons, as well as the unsolved murders of marginalized women, girls, and femme-presenting people in the United States, we don't have a concrete idea of the femicide rate in this country.

We know that of documented murders, 22 percent of the nearly fifteen thousand people killed every year in the United States are women, while only 11 percent of the murders in El Salvador are women. Although Canada's overall murder rate is lower than that of the United States', 30 percent of victims in Canada are women. Despite narratives that position other countries as less civilized and more dangerous for women and girls than the West, the reality is that rates of violence are among the worst in the world here.

For those with disabilities, the very caregivers they have to rely on may be their greatest threat. Though there are many committed caregivers out there doing a wonderful job of supporting loved ones, many disabled women and children are vulnerable to violence precisely because they are dependent on someone who may be taking advantage of them. Caregivers who care more about their own comfort and convenience than the basic rights and welfare of their charges are a dangerous necessity for many people who don't have any other options.

These might come in the form of a family member experiencing fatigue, one with limited or nonexistent empathy, or a paid employee who's there for the money, but not particularly concerned or otherwise invested in the welfare of their patient. Not only do disabled women in abusive relationships, whether it be with a romantic partner, a family member, or an employee, report the horror of losing control over access to food, bathing mobility, and their community, but some are being used solely for the minimal income that they may bring in from social services programs. An unbalanced power dynamic plus a lack of alternative care options can leave victims feeling trapped in situations that are ultimately dangerous.

Because of a societal bias toward sympathetic portrayals of the able-bodied caregiver, even when the outcome is the violent end of a person's life, there is an unwillingness to see that these deaths are part of an epidemic of violence against women and children. Disability activist groups that attempt to draw attention to the problem and get the laws changed to better insulate people from abusive caregivers are facing an uphill battle.

Any chance of successfully combating this problem lies in the government's willingness to follow the lead of the communities most impacted. Yet these are the same communities that have the most to fear from the police, and who are least likely to be respected, much less given adequate resources. This is especially obvious when the targets of violence are trans or nonbinary.

Trans people in the United States are facing increasing rates of violence as new reports reveal more murders and deaths of trans people than ever previously reported. Because of flaws in the way gender is recorded in statistics around violence, and because transphobic families are sometimes reluctant to report a gender identity that differs from the identity that is assigned at birth, any numbers are at best a small sample of those who have been lost.

Some trans women, like CeCe McDonald, have successfully fought attackers off and saved themselves, but at a high personal cost. After CeCe and her friends were accosted by three drunk people outside a bar in Minneapolis, CeCe was struck in the face with a glass, resulting in facial lacerations that needed stitches. When she attempted to run away, Dean Schmitz chased her and she ended up stabbing him. He died and CeCe McDonald was charged with second-degree murder. Though CeCe struck a plea deal and was ultimately sentenced to forty-one months in jail for second-degree manslaughter, the reality is that her fear was legitimate. Many trans women have not survived similar assaults, and nearly 90 percent of the trans people who have been killed were people of color. Yet self-defense can lead to imprisonment if you don't fit into a convenient victim narrative. Look at the case of Cyntoia Brown, a woman facing fifty-one years in jail for killing a man who was sexually abusing her. Prosecutors and media imagery rendered a sixteen-year-old girl as a conniving adult woman engaged in sex work as though the idea that she had been trafficked and abused was anathema. These are cases where we at least have an idea of what happened. For many, they go missing and minimal police resources are committed to finding them.

Even when the missing are underage, and thus should be part of an Amber alert, if police assume they are runaways, that can prevent an Amber alert from being distributed until it is far too late. The reasons people go missing can range from illness to accident to interpersonal danger, with causes ranging from escaping domestic violence to human trafficking to serial killers; the variety is an obstacle to disappearances being investigated, much less solved, in any community.

Add in a pattern of media and police indifference, racism, lack of resources, and complicated jurisdictional issues between tribal, federal, and local law enforcement agencies, and the reasons the problem isn't being addressed in a holistic way become clear. But instead of individual groups having to each plead for resources for their community, what might addressing these issues look like if everyone had access to the kind of resources usually devoted to missing white women? What if this was framed as everyone's problem, not one relegated to the margins of society?

This doesn't mean that white women who go missing don't deserve every bit of attention, care, and concern from the public, police, and the press. It does mean that the same level of concern should be given to all. And this is an approach that can only help those in danger if they know that they have somewhere to turn. It will make predators less likely to target anyone if they know that there are no communities that will be ignored.

Currently many of those who are responsible for the serial

victimization of marginalized women likely feel that they have identified the perfect victim pool. Whether they target people with substance abuse issues, homeless people, or sex workers, they know that the chances of those types of people getting as much attention as a cheerleader or a soccer mom are minimal. That doesn't mean that sex workers or anyone else in a marginalized position is worth less, loved less, or missed less by those who knew them. It means that we have an appalling narrative about which victims are worthy.

It's disturbing enough that the people who are easiest for us as a society to accept as victims are femme presenting. We expect cis women and girls to be harmed, so we focus our energy on warning them to avoid danger. We are less likely to even see them as victims if they don't perfectly adhere to an arbitrary set of behavioral standards we assume can reduce risk. It's maddening when you realize class and race further impact which victims are seen at all. And it's true that we don't know if missing-persons coverage helps resolve cases. After all, even with regular and ongoing coverage, some missing people are simply never found at all. But equitable representation in media coverage matters because that attention shapes how we perceive who has value, and often dictates to whom people will extend their sympathies.

When faced with the disappearance of a loved one, in addition to the emotional anguish of not knowing the missing person's fate, the friends and families of the missing often have to deal with the social, economic, and legal implications of these disappearances, and they do so without any real support in the long term because of socioeconomic circumstances that are highly discriminatory. The possibility that a loved one had a criminal record, a history with drugs, or some other aspect of their life that renders them an imperfect victim can color not only what happens in the immediate aftermath but also what resources loved ones can access over time.

Families may not feel able to get involved earlier in the process of bringing attention to their missing loved ones because they don't know how to go about engaging the media, and instead end up waiting to be contacted. Families may be reluctant to push for answers because of feelings of shame and embarrassment when circumstances around the disappearance involve crime, sex trafficking, and drugs. As a result of that lack of media and family pressure and because of implicit bias, staff at overworked and underfunded agencies may feel justified in giving more attention to cases involving white victims.

Meanwhile gender-based violence is clearly a feminist issue, yet it is a place where race and class have not only divided resources and media, but a range of -isms divide the responses to those at risk. Whether it is transphobia, anti-Blackness, Islamophobia, or xenophobia, there isn't anything approaching a unified effective response to gender-based violence that is inclusive of all.

Obviously, there is no quick and easy solution to a crisis that is global and complicated, but there has to begin to be a conversation beyond carceral solutions like the Violence Against Women Act. Punishment after the fact for a small percentage of offenders isn't going to dissuade any predators. Instead, what is going to continue to happen is that offenders will choose those who are least likely to be protected, not unlike a lion picking off the weakest member of a herd of gazelles. In the face of this kind of violence, we have to be willing to work together; we have to be willing to stand and fight together.

Perhaps the best example of what I have in mind is found in the solutions that some women in India and Kenya who were victims of gender-based violence have found. They band together, prioritizing their safety above broader societal narratives about the need for a patriarch to protect them. True feminist solidarity across racial lines means being willing to protect each other, speaking up when the missing women are not from your community, and calling out the ways that predatory violence can span multiple communities. We must confront the dangers in our own communities, schools, and churches, in order to address this crisis. We have to invest in truly being our sister's keeper. To take action when we see each other in trouble and step in to back those who are forced to defend themselves with violence as well.

Carceral solutions to violence are a complicated topic. It's easy to think of arresting predators as a solution, yet laws that govern the state's response to violence are more likely to be used against victims than against villains. And there's the sad fact that respectability dynamics don't just impact how the state responds to reports that someone is missing; they impact how the state responds to those who may have harmed them. But when we center on the safety of those who are most vulnerable to violence, when we make it a priority to prevent violence from occurring or escalating, then there's a greater chance of a cultural shift toward reducing the danger to all. This is where we fall into the sticky, hard work of challenging not just the ownership narratives propagated by the patriarchy but also into the harder work of undoing the cultural messaging that privileges predators until they have done grievous harm.

We have to be willing to use violence diversion programs more liberally than we use probation, have to have a program that starts in school to unteach the normalization of violence against women.

FEAR AND FEMINISM

In college, I took a class called the Psychology of Sexual Harassment, taught by a woman by the name of Dr. Louise Fitzgerald. It was a good class filled with information that helped me later when I was sexually harassed at work. It couldn't protect me, but it could prepare me, and for that I am grateful. What I remember most about that class was the day a white girl piped up as we were talking about Anita Hill and asked, "Why do Black women always support Black men?" She was offended that more Black women hadn't acted in what she perceived as a feminist fashion and rallied to support Anita Hill. She ignored (or more likely didn't know) that many Black women *had* rallied behind Hill. What she knew was that all the faces she saw supporting Hill were white women, and for several long, aggravating moments, she attempted to craft a narrative about male privilege and patriarchal attitudes that was completely race blind. It fell apart under the barrage of facts that followed from me, from the Black male TA, and even from one of the other white girls in the class.

In retrospect, it was probably a little upsetting for her, being challenged by so many people at once. We brought up not only the support of Black women for Anita Hill but also media narratives, racism, and the danger of assuming that her memory of a snippet of history was the whole story. At best the conversation was spirited, more likely it felt hostile, and yet the doorway to hostility wasn't opened by the people challenging her assertions. Her question lacked nuance; her follow-up comments laid bare her belief that somehow Black women weren't doing feminism right because it didn't look the way she expected. And woven throughout the conversation was her own unexamined racism in assuming that white feminism held the answers for Black communities.

It was an unremarkable moment in some ways, because none of her attitudes were uncommon. She was all set to fight the patriarchy and was certain that there was only one correct way to do that. The patriarchy sounds like a monolithic entity until you consider the reality that men of color don't have the power to oppress in the same way that white men do. I wonder if, in the wake of the confirmation hearings of Justice Brett Kavanaugh, whose nomination to the Supreme Court was called into question when allegations of sexual assault surfaced against him, as well as in the aftermath of the 2016 election of Donald Trump, who has become infamous for his sexism, she asks herself the same questions about white women. Where, across the years, have white women called each other out for failing to confront the impact of white patriarchal systems? Where are the account-ability measures to address the ways that white women have been complicit in the oppression of other women by those white male patriarchal people and systems?

White women, mothers of daughters, have stepped forward to justify predatory behavior by claiming "groping is no big deal." They have marched and held signs defending both Trump and Kavanaugh. Amid reports about Kavanaugh's temperament being unsuitable for the highest court in the land, stories that reflect a history of issues with self-control have been met with an almost cavalier lack of interest in the potential consequences of giving someone unfit so much power. In a response to stories about Supreme Court Justice Kavanaugh getting into bar fights as an undergrad, prominent Canadian journalist and right-leaning cen-trist political pundit Jen Gerson argued on Twitter, "My position on bar fights: A relatively small number of men possess the tem-peramental bent to engage in a bar fight. These men can be prob-lems. But you wouldn't want to be stuck in a zombie apocalypse without such men. They are problems we are stuck with."

It almost sounds like a logical response until you remember that we're talking about the Supreme Court, not the apocalypse. And even if we were talking about a zombie apocalypse as a real possibility, you don't want the hotheaded, short-tempered po-tential rapists with you for the apocalypse. At best they would be a danger to you; at worst they would use you to shield them-selves. It's the kind of no-win situation that can only be avoided by refusing to be a handmaiden of the patriarchy. Well, at least that wouldn't be in my plans. Yet, here we are with women who benefit from mainstream feminism doing all the work of the patriarchy to undermine their own rights and freedoms.

Mainstream, white-centered feminism hasn't just failed women of color, it has failed white women. It's not making them any safer, any more powerful, or even any wiser. It supports the goals of white supremacy so often and so uncritically that 53 percent of white women voted not just for the idea of a president who has a legacy of disrespecting and abusing women, but for the system that supports him. Conditions aren't getting better for white women; in fact these patterns reflect a return to a paradigm where the only difference is that their cage is gilded, while others are entrapped in less decorative confines.

It's easy to say, "Well those weren't feminists," and pretend that feminism is something that is only accessible to liberals, but the reality is that we got to a government that debates the right to choose, the value of women in the workforce, and whether being a rapist is a reason to disqualify someone from the highest offices in the land because feminism empowers all women without really engaging with what that can mean for marginalized people. It's bad enough that white women won't even vote to protect themselves; what's worse is that as a voting bloc they have enough power to harm others. Senator Susan Collins from Maine is a white woman who owes her position to the advances won by feminism. Yet, even though she's pro-choice, she still opted to confirm Justice Kavanaugh, despite clear evidence that he is anti-choice.

Conservative feminists figure out reasons to justify why they deserve equality and safety at the expense of others. Professor

Christina Hoff Sommers, author of *Who Stole Feminism? How Women Have Betrayed Women* and *The War Against Boys*, routinely argues against policies that aid girls and women socially, while claiming to be a real feminist because she's not interested in gender but in equity. Her idea of equity doesn't include addressing the structural problems of sexism because now that she has succeeded in getting what she wants, she seems curiously unconcerned with the lives of other women who are not like her. When Karin Agness started the Network of Enlightened Women on college campuses in 2004, the stated goal was intellectual diversity, but in execution the focus has been on recognizing men's "achievement" in being gentlemen on campus, victim blaming, and protesting performances of *The Vagina Monologues*. It's not feminism for all women, just for those who think they can be safe inside a patriarchal white supremacist society. It requires no empathy, compassion, care, or concern, and yet it is still technically feminism. Conservative feminism enables some of the worst policy decisions under the guise of women protecting women.

Whether their justification is being against abortion or the misguided belief that the racism and sexism espoused by the GOP are harmless, they are happy to benefit from feminism and affirmative action while undermining the very concepts that gave them access to power. Ultimately any argument that they are somehow separate from mainstream white feminism ignores not only the numbers in terms of votes but also the ways that mainstream feminism will rush to bolster and defend them. When Alabama passed the most restrictive anti-choice legislation since *Roe v. Wade* was enacted, it was not white men who were responsible. State rep Terri Collins wrote the bill, and Governor Kay Ivey is ready to sign it. They're conservative women who have been empowered by feminism to do harm.

When Megyn Kelly was being castigated by some of Trump's supporters for daring to ask him about his misogynistic language toward women, there was a push to rally around her, to protect this new "brave feminist" voice. The fact that Kelly made her name by way of the most perplexing casual racism (sternly arguing that Santa Claus was white, for example) and other Fox News–friendly bigotry was suddenly swept away in a tide of one-way sisterhood. Kelly changed absolutely nothing about her politics, while she rode a moment of quasi-feminist behavior all the way to a better job with a broader reach. She promptly dropped any pretense of learning from her experiences with misogyny, then resumed her original pattern of supporting a white supremacist ideology that leaves no space for women who are not like her to achieve more than a limited measure of success. Ultimately it wasn't her criticism of Trump that got her fired, nor was it any advocacy for the rights of women. Kelly's career on daytime TV ended as it began: in racism. This time, though, it was an ardent defense of blackface mixed with plummeting ratings that took her off the air.

You can argue that conservative values are at odds with feminist ideology, but ultimately the question has to be not only "What women are we empowering?" but also "What are we empowering them to do?" White women aren't just passive beneficiaries of racist oppression, they are active participants. White women have long been the bedrock of conservative ideology in

America, from Phyllis Schlafly's attacks on the Equal Rights Amendment to current antiabortion pushes. For white, mainstream feminism the arguments are further left politically, but still exclusionary.

Whether it is Abigail Fisher suing to undermine affirmative action or Sheryl Sandberg leaning into Facebook's pandering to alt-right conspiracy theories, the reality is that white, mainstream feminism has to confront the idea that the power to do harm rests in women too. We can't simply pretend that the politics that unfold around the impact of feminism aren't informed by the greater world. Case in point, the recent proliferation of white women calling the police on Black and Brown people for reasons that run the gamut from eating lunch to being in a parking lot. Feminism has told these women they have a right to occupy every space, but it has not passed on the message that they don't have a right to force everyone else to comply with their whims.

When everyone was celebrating how peaceful the Women's March was and posting pictures of white women in pink pussy hats posing with cops, there was a seemingly sincere attitude of "See, this is how you do protests," which was in stark contrast to the way Black Lives Matter protests have been met with cops in riot gear, dogs, and worse. Challenging the patriarchy too often stops at challenging the ways it is used against other women and their communities. Racism has permeated feminism to such an extent that even when white feminism should be making common cause against white supremacy, white feminists are instead being validated in their fear of people of color, especially Black people. Instead of questioning themselves or the narratives they've been taught, they fall back on the familiar. They have been taught that the police are there to protect, and they forget or outright ignore that while the police may rush to a white woman's defense, for many women, the police and the state in general are a source of violence.

Too often white women decide that when they feel uncomfortable, upset, or threatened, they can turn to the patriarchy for protection. Because they don't want to lose that protection (dubious as it is), they stand by it when it's convenient, and challenge it only when it directly threatens them. Yet, they know they benefit from it being challenged, and thus rely on others to do the heaviest lifting. They fail to recognize that the conflicted relationship they have with the patriarchy includes a certain cowardice around challenging not only it, but other women who have embraced it.

Yet when white women see women of color conflicted about the behaviors of men in their own communities, when they observe women of color not publicly hashing out every single feeling in the way that white women think they should, they are often quick to critique women of color. There's a certain license to assume that somehow feminism is the province of white women who choose to share it with others instead of the work of all toward equality if not equity. It's a myth that not only lets them cluck disapprovingly at flaws in communities that they don't belong to, but also gives them a pass to pretend that their communities are somehow healthier or safer.

When white women pathologize the problems in communities of color while ignoring the danger that they face from the white male patriarchy, they create a framework where they need people of color, especially Black women, to be perfect representations of a brave feminism they refuse to embody themselves. Offended by our focus on our own communities, they cannot fathom that we are dealing with complex situations on our own terms. They balk at the idea that we have ownership over ourselves, that whether it is our bodies, our lives, or our children on the line, our priority is protecting whole communities and that we expect them to do the same.

Does this mean that women in the hood don't have to challenge patriarchal ideas? Absolutely not. It does mean a curious balancing act that often requires solutions outside the carceral state. When you know that oppression comes not from one direction but from many, then you have to develop a framework that allows for not finding safety or solidarity with those who oppress people who look like you.

For women from marginalized communities, that can mean never calling the police because you know that stopping one form of violence by introducing another isn't safe for you or for those you love. There's an idea that the ways that women of color interrogate each other's actions and motives can seem aggressive. But without that step, without those challenges, someone who needs help can wind up dead at the hands of police.

Intervention inside communities is often interpersonal: a call, a conversation, sometimes a fight. It's imperfect and messy. But solutions that actually help the community in the long term are often thin on the ground. If white feminism is a weapon, then intersectional feminism is a pressure bandage. It can't heal the wounds, but it can stop the bleeding and give a community a chance to heal on its own.

Feminism that comes from a place of fear, that prioritizes not being afraid or not being uncomfortable over being effective, is dangerous. It allows no room for considering the impact of some "feminist" choices that include increasing surveillance or inviting the state into spaces in ways that render those spaces fundamentally unsafe for some. The fear of alienating other white women by refusing to challenge them or deny them support as a consequence for their racism is fundamentally damaging to any concept of feminism as a place that can create safety for all.

When we talk about the dangers of white supremacy, we tend to do so around the idea that the anger of white men is inherently dangerous, while ignoring how often that anger is directed and weaponized via the fears of white women. White women's fears can undermine the futures of whole communities. Much is made of the "scariness" of the anger that comes from marginalized people, and every time feminism fails to challenge that fear, every time it feeds into the narrative that fear is a reason to uphold white supremacist structures, feminism fails at the very basic step of advocating for equality.

Does that mean fear is an invalid emotion? Of course not, but there comes a point when fear has clearly overridden logic and is causing more problems than it can possibly solve. Just as fear of a Black man was used to justify lynching, fear of offending other white women has become the excuse for not confronting the harm white women are doing to themselves in their haste to uphold the limited protections offered by white privilege.

Fear—real, bone-deep fear of the harm that can be done by putting someone like Kavanaugh on the bench—is derided until the consequences show up. If people on the right fear change, the patriarchy fears equality, and some white feminists fear equity, then what do marginalized people fear? And how are they coping with that fear? It isn't by voting for the worst possible candidates in droves; it certainly isn't by refusing to confront what's wrong in their communities or outside them. Every community has people who pick the status quo over the risks inherent in fighting for freedom. But the peculiar impact of white fragility on the dynamics between white women means that too often mainstream white feminists get hung up on being polite at the expense of being effective.

It isn't just Kavanaugh or the other judges like him—the ones with a history that clouds their ability to render anything like justice—that's the problem. It isn't just the mothers willing to render their daughters as disposable to protect the sons of the privileged. It is all the ways that the problem is either ignored or poorly addressed until it is a public crisis because white women often choose race over gender based on fear stoked by bigotry. It's the harm that this fearful mind-set can do across communities. Fear of Black people. Fear of immigrants. Fear of the Other. It's an endless cycle that hinges on the willingness of white women to ignore their own power to effect positive change.

While it may be true that some white women are swayed by the opinions of their fathers, husbands, sons, and pastors, for the most part, white women have the agency and autonomy to sway their families away from these narratives that tradition trumps all, and toward a better future. Instead of rallying behind narratives that center on America's return to the misogynistic past, they could actually vote in their own interests. They could skip the dramatic shows of support for predators and instead support their own freedoms.

Irrationally, what white women seem to fear is that if they push back against the misogyny, then what power they currently have will be lost. In the same way that many white men seem to see power as a zero-sum game, so white women want to cling to the agency and selfhood they feel they have fought so hard to achieve. They genuinely believe that by defending these avatars of the patriarchy, they will somehow benefit even if it is at the expense of everyone else.

When you see casual racism from so-called feminist white women, you have to understand that whatever work they are willing to do to insulate themselves, they are still willing to sacrifice others for their right to be equal oppressors. They might not characterize it that way, might feel genuinely offended that anyone can perceive them as a weak link in the chain that is feminism. But realistically, the work that needs to be done internally is less about overcoming the white male patriarchy and more about giving up their embrace of it.

White supremacy isn't just about normalizing racism, but when white women help to maintain the status quo in a society that is dripping with white supremacy, they give themselves more power. Furthermore, because white women have historically centered their own concerns in every movement, their priorities have largely revolved around keeping themselves intact, safe, and free.

RACE, POVERTY,
AND POLITICS

I was sixteen years old and a senior in high school when Bill Clinton was first elected president in 1992. And even then, two years before I was old enough to vote, I understood that being better than the last Republican wasn't the same as being good for everyone. Mixed in with his folksy everyman shtick, saxophone playing, and pronouncements about not inhaling, there seemed to be a tacit promise that President Bill Clinton would govern in ways that actually helped every American. Yet the first Clinton administration was almost as aggressively anti-poor people as Ronald Reagan's administration a decade prior. Between Clinton's "Welfare to Work" bill and the gutting of other social safety nets, it was clear that ending poverty wasn't actually a priority for his administration. I wasn't a fan of Bill Clinton as president, and to be honest, I wasn't particularly en-amored with the idea of Hillary Clinton as president either. I'm a peculiar specimen, someone who lives in a state where political parties don't seem to matter when it comes to political corruption. I was poor in the wake of welfare reform, you see, and while there were programs to help, you could see already that welfare reform was more about punishing poverty than ending it.

Poverty is an apocalypse in slow motion, inexorable and generational. Sometimes a personal apocalypse, sometimes one that ruins a whole community. It isn't a single event of biblical proportions, but it is a series of encounters with one or more of the fabled Four Horsemen. When politicians talk about the working class and the rust belt, we can hear that they understand the consequences of long-term poverty. They can grasp that it isn't a moral failing or a personal failing, but instead the consequences of bad policy and limited opportunity colliding over time. But when it comes to the inner city, suddenly the morality of poverty must be debated. The idea that working-class people live there suddenly vanishes despite the city functions relying on those populations. Voter suppression collides with voter disinterest to further the disenfranchisement of residents. It's this recipe that lends itself to the political landscape in America and elsewhere trending further and further to the right, where the belief in bootstrap logic dominates policy making even in the Democratic party.

There's a blithe assumption that low voter turnout is about laziness or a lack of information or motivation. It almost never comes up in political discourse during an election cycle that for those living in decaying neighborhoods, the years of neglect have left the impression that party doesn't matter, that no politician cares enough to try to stem the tide. Nor do we address the way that having a front-row seat to the brutality of poverty and neglect can impact a person emotionally. Yet millions of women live right there; they grow up on that precipice, raise children there, and have to navigate life in the shadow of potential destruction.

When we frame the working class as only being white people in rural areas, when we talk about the economic anxieties of that group as justification for their votes in 2016 and 2017, we ignore the very real harm done not only to inner-city communities of color, but to all communities of color here and abroad. From the way multiple American administrations have used deportation to force out immigrants to the way the Trump administration has used not only deportation but outright jailing of asylum seekers, the poor are suffering. Outside US borders, US foreign policy increasingly privileges the wealthy at the expense of the poor. American imperialism has always enabled dictators to access and retain power if it serves Western interests, and now under Trump we have stopped even paying lip service to the idea of the greater good.

When some bigoted white people heard the message of Donald Trump and others in the GOP that their concerns mattered, that the fear generated by their own biases had a target in Mexican and Muslim immigrants, many embraced the GOP to their own detriment. We talk at length about the 53 percent of white women who supported the Republican candidate for president, but we tend to skim past the reality that many white voters had been overtly or passively supporting the same problematic candidates and policies for decades.

Researchers point to anger and disappointment among some whites as a result of crises like rising death rates from suicide, drugs, and alcohol; the decline in available jobs for those who lack a college degree; and the ongoing myth that white people are unfairly treated by policies designed to level the playing field for other groups—policies like affirmative action. Other studies have pointed to the appeal of authoritarianism, or plain old racism and sexism.

Political scientist Diana Mutz said in an interview in *Pacific Standard* magazine that some voters who switched parties to vote for Trump were motivated by the possibility of a fall in social status: "In short, they feared that they were in the process of losing their previously privileged positions." Instead of taking rising college enrollment rates by marginalized people as a sign that they would need to improve their own skills, they voted based on a fear they were losing their privilege and thus their positions. This voting phenomenon isn't just about money or racism or sexism, it is about all of the above, and in many ways, the problem exists because of a refusal to reckon with American history. Americans love the myth of a meritocracy more than anything else, because it lets us ignore the reality of the impact of bigotry.

This backlash immediately following Barack Obama's presidency is hardly unexpected. The idea (and the reality) of Black success has always triggered some level of anger in American society. Reconstruction efforts after the Civil War were stymied by racism. Despite the idea of freedom and equality for all being a significant part of American ideals, in execution American society relies on anti-Blackness and inequality. After all, despite the significant overlap between activists involved in abolitionism and women's rights, the history of the women's suffrage movement includes a clear goal of maintaining white supremacy by giving white women equal power with white men.

White supremacist assertions by white suffragettes like Laura Clay, who was cofounder and first president of the Kentucky Equal Rights Association, are nothing new. Upon considering how the vote in the hands of Black people could threaten white dominance, she stated, "The white men, reinforced by the educated white women, could 'snow under' the Negro vote in every State, and the white race would maintain its supremacy without corrupting or intimidating the Negroes." Consider also Belle Kearney, a suffragist, white supremacist, and the first woman elected to the Mississippi State Senate, who maintained:

> The enfranchisement of women would insure immediate and durable white supremacy, honestly attained, for upon unquestioned authority it is stated that in every southern State but one there are more educated women than all the illiterate voters, white and black, native and foreign, combined. As you probably know, of all the women in the South who can read and write, ten out of every eleven are white. When it comes to the proportion of property between the races, that of the white outweighs that of the black immeasurably.

Fast-forward one hundred years, and under the claims of economic anxiety, it's clear that white Trump voters were largely driven by racial resentment, regardless of their gender. But what was most damning was how many white women who had benefited from the advances of feminism and affirmative action rushed to help undermine the same policies that gave them power and freedom.

Their subsequent support of other deeply flawed candidates continued to reflect the reality that facts and finances had very little to do with the success of racist and sexist candidates. The bombastic promises to bring back coal and to "make America great again" were a thin veneer of false hope over a gleefully racist cruelty. It was a long con that seemed to draw out the most ridiculous examples of how difficult it is to reconcile the ideals of equality with the reality of the consequences of racism. The idea that America's greatness rested on Jim Crow–era myths is appealing to many because they still believe in white supremacy despite all evidence to the contrary. Adding to the numbers of powerful white women in no way ensures that the additions will back policies or candidates that are good for all women.

Take the performances that marked Justice Kavanaugh's rise to the Supreme Court. Images of white women wearing "I stand with Brett" and "Women for Kavanaugh" T-shirts filled the airwaves during the hearings. Though there were plenty of white men included in his support system (men who famously outnumbered women in one photo op for the "Women for Kavanaugh" buses), the sight of a group of ten to fifteen women confidently cutting a path through the protesters to show support for a candidate likely to undermine access not only to reproductive justice, but to health care in general, was jarring. They ranged in age from maiden to crone, and yet none of them seemed wise enough to grasp that they were arranging themselves solidly against the rights of all women in favor of propping up the patriarchy. And it's not just an issue on the right—many of Bernie Sanders's most fervent supporters were seemingly convinced that verbally attacking anyone of color who criticized him was good politics.

Bernie Bros was the name given to this mix of real supporters and trolls who seemed to haunt social media platforms specifically to aggressively berate anyone who was not a Bernie supporter. Although some Sanders supporters insisted that the Bernie Bros weren't real, that they were all trolls, and that the term erased women who supported Bernie, the reality was that the term wasn't the problem. The problem was that theoretically leftist supporters of Sanders felt comfortable calling Black and Brown voters "low information" for not supporting their preferred candidate.

Overall, surveys found that while 40 percent of voters opposed Kavanaugh's confirmation, the number of Republican women supporting him rose to 69 percent in the days after he and Dr. Christine Blasey Ford testified.

For many Republican supporters, Kavanaugh's testimony came across as forceful instead of the frightening rant that it was. Some pundits and politicians split hairs, arguing that while they believed Dr. Ford, they didn't believe that her assailant was Justice Kavanaugh, an argument that defied all logic. Whatever the reason, one thing is clear: partisan politics fueled by bigotry overruled reason and allowed many to support not only a president (who has been accused of sexual assault and misconduct by almost twenty women) but a party that only pays lip service to caring about women while enfranchising a standard devoted to undermining not just Dr. Ford's credibility, but that of any woman who dares to speak up against powerful men.

It might seem shocking that an educated white woman wasn't able to stop Kavanaugh's confirmation even with the support of major mainstream feminist organizations. But their willingness to ignore the "wrong" victims based on race or gender or class paved the way to this moment. When some victims are seen as disposable, then eventually all victims are disposable, regardless of white supremacist patriarchal claims to be invested in the protection of white womanhood. It's not enough to show up for the big battles; unfortunately feminism has to show up for every battle, or it can rapidly find itself nearly powerless to prevent moments like these.

The political power of white women in particular is rarely treated in the same way as that of other groups. Despite the expectation that Black or Latinx or Asian voters be treated as a monolith, no one really expects white women to vote as a unified bloc. This is especially obvious after all the elections that prove giving white women the right to vote has, in fact, worked to preserve wide swaths of white privilege. Why? Because white supremacist women have always existed and feel no allegiance to anything but racism.

Meanwhile for voters of color, especially Black women, who are often expected in American politics to save everyone else, there isn't even the pretense that their votes can actually be cast in their own best interests, or that they might have different ideas of what their interests are than what candidates insist they should be. There are no politicians running in any election who prioritize the concerns and needs of the poorest and most vulnerable. Lip service is paid to the idea, of course, but in execution, American politics and American politicians are largely responsive to money. Space is often given to the idea that what helps those with the most money will help those with the least. Yet we know that there is no such thing as trickle-down wealth, much less an effective top-down approach to helping the community. Being led by those with the least sounds counterintuitive, but in reality, the old adage about a rising tide lifting all boats is ironically an apt metaphor for what could be happening if white women voted largely like Black women.

This is not to say Black women are automatically better prepared or better versed in politics. In fact, what is most common is that the poorest people are the best versed in what it takes to survive. As a result, their focus is less on fattening the pockets of the rich and is instead on what will keep the lights on and the kids fed, and allow for at least a few small pleasures. There comes a point—when you have never had anything—where you don't begrudge your neighbors having as much as you, because you know that if you work together, then you can survive hard times together. It's less about altruism and more about simple math. Keeping up with the Joneses is way down on the priority list when you know that the Joneses are likely to share whatever they have if you need help.

If you don't have the resources to get through the month on your own, but sharing resources with your friend or neighbor means you both make it, then of course you want everyone to have more. We frame politics and voting as a zero-sum game that must be won by one side, when it is in fact always about harm reduction. The lack of empathy on display in any given political party for the other would be funny if the consequences weren't so dire.

In a country where Republican senator Cindy Hyde-Smith made coy jokes about lynching and still won an election in a state that is 44 percent Black, the question shouldn't be "How are Black people voting?" It should be "What can we do to change the way white people are voting?" Or better yet, "How do we protect voting access?" For marginalized people, feminism is failing them by being so focused on whether middle-class white women have what they need and want, but not on protecting voting rights for everyone else. This isn't just a problem for Americans—after all, if candidates and their supporters can't see people of color inside the United States as human beings worthy of protection and support, then what chance do those outside the country have?

Dehumanization is the first step in justifying voting against the rights of other people. This is true here in the United States and everywhere else. When you have the kind of military power that this country boasts, voting solely on personal interests with no concern for the wider impact is inherently selfish, and in the case of voting for white supremacy, it's inherently self-loathing, because whatever consequences other communities face will eventually land at your door too.

As much as I didn't want to vote for another Clinton, I had already reconciled myself to the idea that the least harmful option was the only one available. In the end, it wasn't the popular vote that mattered so much as it was the electoral college, and that is perhaps the most damning part of any discussion of race and politics. Even though the popular meme is that Black women voters can make all the difference, the reality is that a coalition of marginalized voters is sometimes not enough to create lasting change.

The fact is that the harm-reducing votes of marginalized people will never be enough to outweigh the stupidity of white people who vote for racism at their own expense. Empathy isn't something that we can expect to teach adults, and as long as white supremacy carries the day in the home and the voting booth for so many white women, the questions about voter turnout are moot in a country where voting rights are under attack. Voter ID laws, attempts to shut down busing voters to polls, and tactics ranging from closing polling centers early to reducing the number of places to get ID in a state are going to undermine voting access for the same groups that helped put Obama and other centrist and progressive leaders in office. From modern-day poll taxes in the form of requiring former felons in Florida to pay all court fines and fees before regaining their voting rights, to registered voters being purged from the rolls, the same old voter-suppression tactics are back in use. Gerrymandering for a segregated school system leads directly to gerrymandering for an anti-choice politician. Just imagine the impact of something like respectability on who has access to the right to vote.

The same views that allowed suffragettes to support white supremacy despite many having been ardent abolitionists are part and parcel of current white feminism ignoring not only the ways that racism impacts elections but also the widening gap between the right to vote and access to voting. The attitudes that we find so abhorrent in suffragettes like Rebecca Latimer Felton, who was the first woman to serve in the United States Senate and is remembered in some circles as a feminist icon despite her support of lynching, underpin carceral feminist logic that ignores one of the main ways that voting rights are being stripped: via discriminatory policing. It's not just Black lives that matter; Black votes matter too. And Black votes are not the only votes in danger. Any woman with a criminal record can lose access to the right to vote.

According to the Sentencing Project's May 2018 report there are approximately 110,000 women incarcerated in America at any given time. That's 1 percent of the total population of women in America. That number has increased significantly since 1980, and with the rise in incarceration rates, many potential voters are being forced out because of laws that make it illegal for convicted felons to vote. The laws change from state to state, and are not rooted in any modern understanding of the impact of the war on drugs on communities of color, much less the impact of police misconduct and brutality. Those most at risk of losing their right to vote are those for whom voting is the only access they have to any semblance of political power.

Is voting the perfect solution to what ails America? Of course not. But having a vote is having a voice in the way the country is run, and sometimes that voice is the first step for a community toward stability and safety.

Long before the 2016 election, mainstream feminism was ignoring the ways that the right to vote was under attack for marginalized people in the United States. The history of voter suppression is well documented. And even though women technically got the right to vote in 1920, realistically, prior to the Voting Rights Act of 1965, states used poll taxes and literacy tests to stop Black and Indigenous people from voting. It was only after multiple lawsuits subsequent to the passing of the act that such obstacles were removed. Politicians in many states immediately started creating new barriers as replacements when those of the Jim Crow era were removed. To this day, some lawmakers continue to pursue policies that would undermine the right to vote. Even though studies have shown that illegal voting is a myth, for the past several years advocates for tougher restrictions on voting have found more support than opposition.

Under the guise of tackling voter fraud, many states adopted measures including strict voter ID requirements and reductions in the number of polling places, especially those with early voting opportunities, to restrict voting ahead of the 2016 election. Most tellingly, several of the states where these early policies were put in place have a long history of racial discrimination in voting, and until recently had to seek federal approval before making any changes in voting laws and procedures. When voting rights advocates pointed out that these measures created barriers for tens of thousands of low-income citizens and citizens of color, the response from the right and the response from much of the left was to ignore both current and historic obstacles to voting for marginalized communities. From right-wing politicians looking to limit voter turnout, that response made sense, but for ostensibly left-leaning politicians to ignore the reasons the Voting Rights Act exists and let it lapse was appalling.

The right to vote is arguably a pillar of American democracy, but countless Americans face barriers to voting. Yet relatively few feminist organizations have made protecting voting rights for all a priority, much less reckoning with the bigotry that allows for so many white women to vote against the interests of all women. Whether it is the women who spoke up to support Kavanaugh's nomination to the Supreme Court only to learn that he had also demeaned and disrespected them, or the Republicans who have surged forward to celebrate his appointment, there are dire consequences for women's rights as a whole because only some women have access to the right to vote.

Any narrative that assumes women can be treated as a united voting bloc with no concern for race, class, or other factors is shortsighted and deeply misguided. The history of feminist politics has shown the dangers of ignoring the work of marginalized women, cis and trans. Frankly, it has been women like Fannie Lou Hamer and Ida B. Wells and so many others who have been leaders across a wide variety of social issues for generations. Their work has done more to improve conditions for all, even though it has been met with minimal recognition or respect from white Americans. Today's feminist movement cannot ignore voting rights for all, not just because the numbers are needed to support causes championed by white women, but because if feminism's goal truly is equality for all, that means the future of feminism has to look very different from its past. Feminism has been a powerful political force for decades, but its focus has to expand if critical elections are going to be won.

Feminism that encompasses all the issues that impact women, from poverty to criminal justice reform to living wages to better protections for immigrants to LGBTQIA issues, is feminism that ensures voting rights for all as a foundational issue.

EDUCATION

Growing up, I remember politicians hopping on TV to talk about how they would save the cities from the "menace" of drug traffickers. It was the age of the "super predator" and we were all supposed to be grateful for leaders who prioritized law and order. But I didn't know any super predators. I knew dopeboys and -girls. The ones who sold drugs, transported them, held them, and sometimes did them. I wasn't one of them—I was a nerd with a future, and despite the tales told in afterschool specials, no one was interested in recruiting me. I was Books to them, and to me they were the same kids I had known since kindergarten.

I understood that while I had my grandparents and aunts and eventually my mother and stepfather around, they had no one, or at least no one who looked at a traumatic situation and did their best to make it better. The boys who sold drugs were largely either in foster care or in kinship care with relatives who could barely afford their own children, much less caring for other people's children, even if they were relatives. At that time, the girls usually didn't sell drugs, though they did transport them, and of course they were involved (often intimately) with the boys and men who were trafficking in green or white. Unlike me, they had no all-seeing grandmother, no grandfather who might pull up at any moment and ask what they were doing.

Instead, they were often the ones responsible for making sure there was food in the fridge or that the gas bill got paid. That responsibility might fall on their shoulders in fifth or tenth grade, or simply have been something that they had always felt was necessary. I have no story about the time I sold drugs, but there are two stories about drug dealers I knew growing up. And how easy it is to need more than you have, and to have no way to get it without resorting to vice. We'll start with Deon J.

Deon was a nice kid. For the first few years of school together, he was just like me and a dozen other kids in our school. He lived in an apartment on Drexel with his grandmother, his sister, and occasionally his mom. Low income, but hanging on like almost everyone else in the neighborhood. Not enough money for all the cool toys and things kids want, but certainly enough to have clothes that didn't stick out, and he was clean and seemingly well fed. He struggled in school when it came to reading, he got teased sometimes for being light skinned or for having Payless shoes. All standard stuff for a 99 percent Black school in the 1980s in Chicago. Kozminski was a segregated school, but we didn't know that, and you can't miss what you never had, so I can't say that any of us really knew what we lacked.

Not having two parents in your home was normal; living with another generation or two was also normal. Families largely pulled together, or so it seemed when we were little. But not every kid had the same support system. When I got sick my grandmother put me to bed, and my grandfather or my aunt supplied the ginger ale or crackers. For Deon, somehow his struggles at home were such that when he had chicken pox in third grade, he mostly roamed the neighborhood while we were in school instead of being home in bed. There was a period in fourth and fifth grade when he had more money for shoes and clothes than anyone else, and by the end of sixth grade it was clear that he was not just hanging around the gangs but was on the road to being in one.

His mom wasn't around much, his grandmother got sick, and he and his sister needed to eat. The rent needed to be paid. The heat needed to stay on. I don't know exactly when he started selling drugs. I do know that at some point his family needed the money he was bringing in more than they needed to keep him on the straight and narrow. He bragged about his place in the hierarchy of the street. As we got older, most of us went to high school, some went to trade school, college, or the military, but Deon stayed on the street. The streets were what he'd been able to rely on. He could take care of his sister and himself even after his grandmother had passed away and his mom stopped her periodic visits. He embraced the streets because they had embraced him when he needed help. I'd see him in passing when I visited my grandmother, and he looked prosperous if not happy most of the time. His sister went on to high school and to college, while he rotated between the streets and jail. I don't know who he could have been, but the streets were all that he would ever have, because they killed him before he was thirty. It's easy to pass judgment on a kid like him, easy to assume that if I made it out so could he, but I had more choices and better resources.

And then there was a girl named LaToya. Same grammar school but she transferred in later; I didn't know her from kindergarten like I did some of the others. She was funny, charming, and surprisingly kind to my nerdy awkward self in seventh and eighth grade. We weren't close, exactly, but I knew her cousins and by proxy her in the years after we left grammar school. She was smart, and probably could have gone on to college. But at some point, LaToya held drugs for her boyfriend. Her mom was dying, the rest of the family wasn't financially stable, and she was a teenager. He paid her and her mother's bills with drug money while she stored the drugs and moved them for him. He was no angel, but he was better than any of her other options, which included the street and what passes for foster care in Illinois and not much else. She did some time when they both got caught, but she was much younger than he was, and if memory serves me correctly, it was her first offense, which meant that she was able to benefit from a now defunct program that helped ex-convicts get back on their feet when they got out of jail. She was able to get a job, a place to live with her kids, and eventually be a "model citizen." With a job, a place to live, and as stable an environment as she can create for herself, she can do anything she wants to do now except vote.

Why this tale of two outcomes? Well, while I didn't get involved in the drug trade because I had some slightly greater measure of familial support and supervision, that doesn't mean I didn't break the law. I trespassed, I shoplifted, I smoked weed, I started drinking alcohol at fourteen, blew curfew, did some petty vandalism. My crimes were more mundane, less likely to arouse police intervention. The hood isn't a hopeless place, but the obstacles that you can face there vary wildly based on mundane factors like whether there's a cop in your school or if you have family who will show up for you early and often.

Every time I got out of line, I did so with the certain knowledge that not only did I need to be sneaky to avoid outside repercussions, but I also needed to stay within the line my grandparents and other relatives set. It was easier to do because I never had to worry about who was going to pay the bills. Or that if something happened to whichever family member I lived with, I would have nowhere to go. When my mother couldn't take care of me, I lived with aunts, my grandparents, or family friends. When my grandfather died during my adolescence, I was living with my mother and stepfather. When my parents and I couldn't get along during my junior and senior years, I could go to a friend's house, back to my grandmother's, or to an aunt's. We all had complicated family dynamics, with parents who were struggling and sometimes failing. Deon had no meaningful adult support and had to be the adult for his sister, LaToya had some support but not always enough, and I had what I needed even if it wasn't always what I wanted.

For all of us, having school staff that cared and a neighborhood that tried to make a difference meant that we could at least imagine a future even when it felt like it was impossible to get there. Deon's story is the saddest for obvious reasons, but as sad as it is, he lived longer than a kid like him would today. Today, he'd be at risk of being shot by police for being a twelve-year-old in a public place with something that might look like a gun. Or he'd have been in handcuffs in school or bludgeoned by a resource officer. In the days before zero-tolerance policies, he was always able to find a safe place at school even if he didn't have one at home. Harsher school policies in the wake of desegregation, and safety practices that include bringing law enforcement into schools have combined to create the school-to-prison pipeline, in which troubled students are subject not just to detention, but to suspensions, expulsion, and even in-school arrests. Instead of counseling or intervention services, schools are increasingly using law enforcement tactics to deal with misbehavior, even for minor incidents.

For the youth who are pushed out of school and into the juvenile criminal justice systems, their futures are more likely to look like Deon's than like mine or LaToya's. This is a feminist and racial justice crisis because the students being pushed out are not only disproportionately students of color, they are increasingly female. Many are also students with disabilities, and that number includes LGBTQIA students as well. Bias doesn't stop at the school door, and the reasons marginalized students are being disproportionately impacted by these policies have more to do with identities than behavior.

Although the idea of zero-tolerance school discipline policies comes from the "tough-on-crime" policies of the 1980s and 1990s, its impact wasn't as severe then, because students were at least likely to be taught by staff who knew them and their families, staff who recognized their fundamental humanity. A lack of teacher diversity combined with unstable school systems, as well as charters that frame a military- or prison-style disciplinary system as the key to student success, can't help but jeopardize student achievement as well as safety. Especially when they are the only options left after dozens of public schools have been closed. When you can be forced out of class for having the wrong colors on your shoes (à la the rules in several charter schools around the country), the adults around you teach you that they value obedience over education. And if they don't value you or your future, then why should you?

The most common form of teacher discrimination manifests in classroom expectations and disciplinary referrals. A biased teacher may end up punishing a particular student more harshly and more often because of the student's identity. They may refuse to use preferred pronouns, write classroom policies that interfere with student access to bathroom facilities, or otherwise create arbitrary standards that guarantee a student will somehow run afoul of the rules. This is especially common for Black and Latinx students in high schools. At sixteen, my oldest child was almost written up his junior year for trespassing by a teacher with whom he had several personality conflicts. The trespassing? He sat in an empty classroom to study before a test. The test was in that classroom. It wasn't his actual teacher who threatened to write him up; his teacher had no problem with it.

The teacher threatening the write-up was likely more interested in control than anything else, but my oldest is smart, challenging, and underwhelmed by petty power displays. There was no real rule against his being in the room, and the door was open, but as far as this teacher was concerned, my son had been caught and deserved punishment. When I asked (as you do) what exactly would warrant a write-up, given how often kids who wanted a quiet place to study did exactly what my son had done, the teacher backed down, claiming he was trying to teach my son some discipline. But since my son was studying, that excuse fell flat. Other ways discrimination from teachers can be seen range from unfair grading to acceptance or encouragement of discriminatory behavior from other students in the classroom.

Missing from discussions of bullying issues in schools is the fact that at least some teachers will be aware of what's happening and will ignore it. As a result, a marginalized student with limited emotional resources may find themselves feeling attacked from all sides. And the problem doesn't stop there. Students who attempt to report discriminatory behavior to the administration may find themselves facing yet another bad actor.

And of course, there's the fact that teachers can also be bullies and use their power over marginalized students in ways that may drive a student out of their classroom, if not out of school altogether. When marginalized students are targeted by teachers, they must contend with feelings of shame and powerlessness. They struggle with establishing other positive relationships within the school. In a 2007 study of students in an alternative school setting, students reported that an adult, rather than a peer, was involved in their worst school experience, with more than 80 percent reporting that they had been physically or psychologically harmed by a teacher. Teacher bullying can also have a contagious effect, indicating to students that the bullying of a particular individual is acceptable and making that individual vulnerable to more abuse. Only recently has teacher bullying of students been identified as a contributing factor to poor outcomes, and while there are studies in progress, there are no hard numbers on how often it is happening.

Perhaps the most distressing aspect of bullying behavior in teachers is how easily it can be explained away by adults who become complicit because they are projecting their own biases onto their students. Parents may know about the behavior through student complaints but think there is nothing they can do except remove their child from that school, because school officials fail to act when it is first reported. Bigoted teachers can even mask their mistreatment of students as part of a legitimate strategy for encouraging achievement. Because of narratives that cite discipline as a reason for achievement gaps, teachers can simply point to the lower grades caused by their own misconduct to justify their actions. When confronted, offenders may minimize or deny the conduct and claim it was a miscommunication. Ignoring the problem of teacher bullying only compounds it. Because inaction supports a hostile environment that undermines learning, parents may find themselves having to combat it in multiple ways. That may mean doing more drop-ins during the school day if possible, having a child carry a recorder or a cell phone, going to the administration, or having to go to the media.

My nine-year-old son had a fourth-grade teacher who was bullying him. At first I thought that my son was overreacting to being lectured about his messy homework, but it increasingly became evident to me that his teacher kept changing the rules about how he should turn in his homework. I spoke with her calmly, and I also spoke with the administration. I even went to the school counselor. Ultimately, the teacher stopped bullying him when my husband and I started popping up outside her classroom. After the first couple of "Surprise, we're right here!" moments, the peculiar behavior stopped. We documented and reported, but like with many bullies, it was only fun for her when her victims couldn't fight back.

Unfortunately, administrator-related discrimination is more common than teacher discrimination. On elementary and high school campuses, administrators may over-penalize students of color while under-penalizing white students for the same behavior. Students from marginalized communities at these schools may be more likely to be suspended or expelled than their majority peers. It's not just a public school problem.

The most common form of racial discrimination in education is harassment of students of color by their white counterparts. Every few days, the news carries a story of racist bullying, whether it be racially motivated physical attacks, racial epithets scrawled on school walls, or organized hateful activities directed at making marginalized students feel unwelcome and unsafe. While isolated incidents by a student on a school campus may not trigger an investigation, repeated offenses or a lack of consequences for offenders when incidents occur can indicate a broader cultural issue. Yet when students of color respond, whether it be through protests or a more direct physical response, they are more likely to have their behavior criminalized by the police officers on staff.

For young women of color, police brutality is already a risk faced from the cradle. There is no Officer Friendly, no safety in an institution that fails to recognize that the errors of young people of color are not inherently more dangerous simply because of the color of their skin. And this attitude of aggressive policing toward students of color is expensive. States spend $5.7 billion a year on the juvenile justice system instead of on our schools. On average, American states spend $88,000 to incarcerate a young person, but allot an average of $10,000 to educate them.

When we think of schools being underfunded, understaffed, and in underserved communities, the math for cops instead of resources simply doesn't make sense. Yet while there's no shortage of educational advocates who benefit from feminism advocating for policy changes that privilege charters over public schools in terms of access to funding, no shortage of middle-class white feminists ready to argue against expanding the boundaries of school districts to include underserved communities, they are often curiously silent about improving conditions in schools in ways that don't include adding more cops.

They falter when the conversation about parental involvement might require them to schedule PTA meetings in ways that are flexible and available to parents who don't have traditional work schedules. Or to confront the bias in school funding and school district lines in ways that might endanger the status quo that privileges predominantly white schools even in cities like Chicago, where the white population is in the minority. We can see these moments play out in real time, when video leaks from school board meetings in New York City show white parents arguing against diversity measures. Or when Asian American parents file lawsuits to stop the process.

FOR MANY PARENTS from marginalized communities, the fight to not only keep schools open but to prevent their children from being criminalized starts as early as preschool. In fact, the money that has been used to increase the number of school officers across the country could be better spent on mental health services to provide counseling for at-risk students and their families. Students need schools and politicians to expand the definition of safety to include more school-based counselors, social workers, nurses, and after-school, weekend, and summer programs.

Calls for increasing school safety rarely acknowledge how policing affects students of color. There's no safety in being profiled, in being surveilled and harassed in a place that should be about opportunities and not total obedience.

We know that inequity permeates the world, in everything from access to clean water to school closures. A prime example of this is the fact that Chicago's school closures between 2002 and 2018 impacted 533 white students, 7,368 Latinx students, and 61,420 Black students. So why isn't access to education a high priority in feminist circles? It certainly isn't from a lack of effort to get attention for the problem.

Activists go to meetings, contact the press, march on state capitols and mayors' offices and sometimes homes. They write letters to editors and stage sit-ins to keep schools open, but overwhelmingly the funding disappears unless and until someone is shilling a "safety plan" that puts an armed person in a school to protect it. We feign shock when those "resource officers" brutalize students or fail to stop a shooting, then turn and bemoan the lack of educational success for students from communities more likely to be policed than educated.

Organizations like Dignity in Schools do their best to track how many kids are being adversely affected. They've found that Black students are suspended and expelled at a rate three times greater than that of white students. Meanwhile, 70 percent of the students arrested or referred to police at school are Black and Latinx. While Black children make up around 16 percent of the K–12 school population in America, they over-index in arrests, comprising approximately 31 percent of school-related arrests. Perhaps most disturbing, students with disabilities are more than twice as likely to receive an out-of-school suspension than students without disabilities. Because there is no consistent process or training for becoming a school police officer, and officers are not always trained on interacting with children and young adults, they may interpret perfectly normal age-appropriate behavior as over-the-top or even criminal behavior.

We know that students in schools with police officers are more likely to get a criminal record, even for nonviolent misbehaviors like vandalism. But what we don't know is how often kids in schools are being brutalized by police, because no one keeps track of those incidents. Oh sure, some make the news, and the resulting public outcry might make changes with that officer in that school. Yet, even in the cases where videos from multiple cities emerged of young Black girls being brutally body slammed by a school officer, mainstream feminist groups barely reacted. Instead, the work of advocating for her rights and the rights of others like her fell solely to racial justice organizations.

It's true that the victims of police brutality in schools, the school-to-prison pipeline, and pushout practices are more likely to be students of color, but that doesn't make it any less of a feminist issue. Welcome to an intersectional feminist approach to education! Those of us who have the option to make safer choices, to be redirected by the community or protected by privilege, must step up and step in to defend these kids from the system that would ruin their lives. We know that some kids are at risk because of situations in their home lives that are the fault of adults. Whether that risk be a result of addiction, poverty, or violence, we cannot let school become an unsafe place.

In general, children from low-income families are at risk of being failed by schools because of the erroneous belief that their parents lack ambition for them. A focus on the need for aspirations is widely cited as necessary for closing the achievement gap between marginalized and privileged people. Yet, in environments where students may not see themselves represented in person or on the page, what exactly are they aspiring to? Who sets those standards, and are they achievable in the wider world without culturally sensitive and competent teachers?

It's not enough for feminism to advocate for educational access; it must also push to make education valuable for all. Quality as well as quantity matter a great deal. It does students no good to be able to go to school if their school is a place where they can be abused and traumatized with impunity by the administration. Challenging the internalized biases that allow the majority white female staff to feel comfortable utilizing police as a weapon against minors in lieu of actual classroom control is necessary to end the school-to-prison pipeline.

We know that sometimes teachers are the bullies; we know that students of color have reported being disciplined for everything from their hairstyles to their accents.

My early home life was tumultuous, and while I certainly never had the middle-class, white picket fence in the suburbs, I was fortunate enough that even when my family situation was deeply unstable, my situation at school was not. When I accidentally set the science lab on fire in eighth grade? Mrs. Archibald made me clean up the mess, but she didn't call the police. When I cut class in the tenth grade to the point of nearly flunking out, I got lectures and interventions, not a trip to juvie. And later when I hung out in all the wrong places, as you do when you're on the edge of taking the wrong turn, it was one of my teachers who told me that all I had to do was hang on until eighteen and then I could determine the course of my life. At every turn I was surrounded by Black teachers who saw me not only as someone with potential, but as someone who deserved a second chance. Whatever you may think of the kids you see on those videos of misconduct in schools, you should ask yourself, *Why are they loud? Why are they angry? Where is their safe space? How has feminism empowered them or their communities? Has it helped those girls at all?* Because ultimately, the ways that we are failing young women of color will come back to haunt their futures and ours.

HOUSING

I've talked about hunger in another chapter, but let's talk for a moment about that other tent peg of poverty, the housing crisis. It's easier in some ways to break it out into separate topics; the scope is less upsetting that way. But the reality is that rising housing costs and lower wages are pushing marginalized women further and further away from stable housing and from personal safety. Budgeting about 30 percent of your monthly income for rent or mortgage costs, as the prevailing wisdom dictates, sounds reasonable until you compare the housing you can afford for 30 percent of a minimum-wage salary with the housing available at that rate.

In theory, public housing and Section 8 programs should be closing the gap—that is, after all, their purpose. Yet families are back to having to share small units in defiance of occupancy codes because of costs. Tetris is a game meant to be played with blocks, not people. And the affordable housing crisis disproportionately impacts women. With the pay gap, women earn less, so they pay more proportionally, and that in turn means households supported by women are paying larger-than-average proportions of income toward rent. We know that the wage gap breaks down by gender and by race, so that white women earn less than white men, and that Black, Latina, and Indigenous women earn less than white women and men. Across a lifetime, this means much lower disposable income, with a higher proportion of earnings spent on housing and greater difficulty achieving financial security and independence.

This is especially clear when you look at people in abusive relationships. Although my story is that of a woman in a heterosexual relationship, the reality is that the housing crisis could affect anyone in an abusive dynamic. It is simply more likely to affect cis and trans women because, although gender isn't binary, there is a financial penalty for presenting as feminine, because misogyny is a hell of a drug.

In 2002 as a newly single parent in college, I cried when I realized that I couldn't afford to keep my apartment. Fortunately, I was able to move into public housing. But government cuts have so negatively impacted funding for housing assistance that Lakeside Terrace, the housing development I lived in for two years post-divorce, is gone now. Section 8 lists in some areas have been closed for decades, and even in areas where those vouchers are available, the rental subsidies for low-income renters have not kept pace with inflation. New properties aren't being built to replace the old ones at nearly the promised rates, and in cities like Chicago the properties are simply sitting empty for years because of reams of red tape and the reality that the people most impacted don't have the political power to effect change.

The housing crisis isn't accidental. It's a direct result of a series of decisions made in many cases by people who are well aware that marginalized people will bear the consequences of those decisions. I was lucky enough to leave my bad relationship when more of these necessary programs still existed. But for many, even if they can leave safely, they can't afford to stay gone. Finding affordable housing isn't just an issue in the hood; even in rural areas, where housing costs are substantially lower than they would be in the nearest urban center, there is a lack of affordable housing. But the sad reality is that lower costs of living go hand in hand with lower income for many in rural areas. Much like conditions for the urban working poor, limited economic opportunities are available for those living and working in depressed areas. For many the housing that they have is unfit for human habitation, but they have no other options. They can complain to absent or nonexistent landlords or the nearest agency, but they run the risk of losing their lease and not being able to secure a new one. Or that landlords will seek an eviction as retaliation. Landlords of that type also continue to let the property deteriorate until it is convenient for them to either make basic repairs or sell the property off.

Low-quality or dangerous housing conditions aren't an anomaly in urban or rural areas. Those who aren't able to save their homes or find new affordable homes are often forced to double up with family members in order to avoid outright homelessness. And unlike with those who end up on the street, that level of homelessness is invisible because people with someplace to go (however tenuous) aren't always counted in the statistics. Many homeless relief programs won't make someone a priority unless they are living in a car, on the street, or someplace else deemed completely unfit.

Matthew Desmond's research for his Pulitzer Prize–winning book on the long-term impact of eviction as a cause of poverty, *Evicted: Poverty and Profit in the American City*, showed that eviction cases in 2016 were filed at the rate of four per minute. As a result of his research, he partnered with Princeton University to create the Eviction Lab, the first nationwide database tracking evictions. Using it, we can see how many people are struggling to stay housed, but even that research, as robust as it is, doesn't allow for a clear picture of how many women have been impacted.

As Desmond points out, housing instability isn't just a result of poverty; it can be the cause of it. Housing is foundational for success, and having it makes it possible for people to go to school or work, care for children, care for elders and for themselves. Yet as housing becomes harder to secure and to maintain because of escalating prices and stagnant wages, the crisis is becoming a catastrophe.

I have been incredibly lucky despite what some friends and I call my housing curse. I've had landlords go into foreclosure, go to jail, die, or simply neglect and mismanage property until it was uninhabitable. I have the knowledge and the resources to solve some of the problems without having to rely on increasingly unstable social safety nets. My husband and I both have college degrees and are hitting the double-income empty-nest stage of life in our forties instead of our fifties or sixties. We have the privilege of financial and social resources.

Despite being a dual-income family, we still faced the possibility of homelessness a few years ago after an apartment we were living in was found to have toxic levels of mold. There's a lot to be said about how easy homelessness is to slip into and how hard it can be to escape. Family shelters are rare, and the lack of emergency housing can leave someone with limited resources in a terrible situation. We had the resources to be hotel homeless, to keep our kids in their schools, and to get a new place almost immediately. And despite having to get rid of most of our possessions because of the mold, we were mostly inconvenienced instead of undone.

It brought home how much privilege I had accrued since my early twenties, when I might not have been able to pull any semblance of stability together. There's nothing exceptional about my stories. I am like millions of women in the hood, in the country, anyplace you can think of where women with less money and the same needs might exist. And yet we don't really talk about the housing crisis as a feminist issue, despite the fact that it primarily impacts women. Oh sure, you can find a handful of articles, perhaps one or two activists bringing it up as a feminist issue. But there are no glitzy campaigns, no programs with catchy slogans backed by famous names. Instead of acting as a collective movement to improve conditions for all, mainstream feminism has largely treated housing as a problem for someone else to solve.

And for those who campaign to bring back affordable housing, to do away with laws that penalize victims of domestic violence, there is a real need for access to power and resources from those who have the privilege of housing stability. Activists who tackle housing insecurity issues are often under-resourced and overworked. And they run right into gentrifiers who pledge to solve the problem by revitalizing neighborhoods with cute little boutiques and coffee shops. The faces of gentrification are often young, white, and female. While the gender pay gap means that white women are unlikely to be able to compete against white men for property in desirable areas, they outearn most other demographics and can afford to take advantage of lower rents and larger spaces in communities of color. Want to start a store that only sells mayo? You can slap a kitschy label on your product, pay far less in rent, and as an added bonus, your presence signals that a neighborhood full of people of color is ripe for economic invasion. We're all on stolen land in the United States, but some communities are far less likely to be impacted by redlining or subprime lending.

In theory, gentrification can bring services and jobs to a community. In practice it means opportunity for some and criminalization for others. It's easy to dismiss claims by residents of increased police presence as speculative when you're new to the area. But for those who have lived through the past few decades in major cities, they have seen the lack of investment in those

neighborhoods as children and later as adults. Even as gentrification has become a norm in major American cities, you can
drive just past the new street planters full of flowers, the boutiques and coffee shops, right into urban blight. In low-income
neighborhoods where longtime residents and businesses are dis-
placed by white-collar workers, you can watch the diversity of
options and people drain away block by block the closer you
get to the center. Along the way you'll also see a difference in
transit options, trash collection, even in the condition of the
road surfaces. The conventional wisdom that gentrification is a
boon because of economic restructuring that brings in more
jobs and resources unfortunately ignores that long-term residents aren't necessarily getting hired, and are often targeted by
new neighbors who don't understand neighborhood norms and
call the police over mundane things ranging from the sound of
ice cream trucks to barbecues. As gentrification rates increase,
criminalization becomes more than a side effect and is instead
a tool that disproportionately affects communities of color. Gentrification forces those residents most in need away from the
new resources and further into blighted areas, where they once
again struggle to access the most basic levels of goods and services.

When desirable low-income neighborhoods see an influx of
higher-income residents and their businesses, social dynamics
and expectations collide. The same congenial chatter from the
stoop on the corner that can be comforting to women of color
is filtered through the lens of street harassment because a man
of color is speaking to a white woman. One of the most telling

examples of this phenomenon was a viral campaign against sexual harassment put on by Hollaback! a few years ago that bizarrely juxtaposed a Latinx man saying hello and a groping attempt by a white man. If you don't remember the campaign, that's no surprise; internet backlash over the unexplained editing out of most white men tanked the campaign within hours of launch. Differing expectations of safety and public order and the role of the state in providing it clash, especially around housing, because while white women might perceive quiet streets and a high police presence as safety, for women of color, this is often a precursor to a violent interaction with agents of the state. For many communities of color, loitering isn't a real crime; it's an excuse for police to harass someone for sitting on a porch or having a cigarette outside the barbershop. For white people from the suburbs, hanging out in the street is apparently a serious issue—as are drummers, people working on cars, and whatever other social behavior can be seen as criminal in racially diverse neighborhoods that are not majority white. And for those who are trying to age in place, the changes can be incredibly disorienting and sometimes dangerous as their community dwindles more rapidly than expected.

Because of the wealth gap, the people most in need of affordable housing in well-resourced areas are least likely to feel welcome there over time. One of my relatives owns a home in the west end of Hyde Park near Washington Square. When she bought it, her home needed renovations, and she got it for a price commensurate with that reality. Fast-forward twenty-three years, and as she settles into retirement and the joys of a nearly paid-off home, she's fielding an obscene number of attempts to get her to sell her property. It's not just the casual "Oh is this house for sale?" No. She's had strangers knock on her door, tell her it is too much house for her, and even write her long-winded letters about how they can picture themselves having brunch on *her* sun porch! The woman who wrote the letter included a wonderful description of her very white-bread middle-American family, complete with a description of herself. Then one day, while we were outside working in the yard, a couple who either matched the description or were the people who wrote the letter came by and asked my aunt how much she charges to do the yard work. It never occurred to them that she was the homeowner. Needless to say, she enjoys knowing that they won't so much as break an egg in her kitchen.

My aunt is lucky; she bought her home for a low price, has been able to keep the taxes paid, and can count on family members to take care of the tasks that might be beyond her physically. She's a homeowner, not a renter who could see their rents double or triple in the face of gentrification while their income stagnates in retirement. As market-rate rents rise, displacement threatens even those who live in protected housing such as subsidized low-income apartments for seniors. Those developments may end up underfunded in any administration, including the current one; they may be shut down and never replaced, as has happened in the past. When residents of these shuttered developments attempt to reenter the rental market, not only are many of their neighbors gone, but they can't afford to stay near the services that they need.

Although most displacement during gentrification occurs through direct means including escalating rents, increased property taxes, or the conversion of modestly priced properties to luxury developments, sometimes it is as simple as removing the rest of the community. Gentrification can trigger indirect displacement that guarantees elders feel alienated in their own community. Younger, whiter residents may bring in cafés and boutiques, but as they push out long-term residents, the changing demographics also undermine local institutions, leaving elders without a pharmacy that delivers, a grocery store that carries staples at an affordable price, and meeting places in parks or elsewhere that are how the neighborhood stays connected. Residents may still be able to afford their housing, but their budget doesn't allow them to feel like they can participate in the world around them. The social death, particularly for older women when they no longer feel connected to the neighborhoods, can be incredibly difficult to manage.

When we talk about housing and feminism, we must remember that it isn't just the concern of the young woman eager to start her business or find a home for her family. It's a concern for older women, for our elders who rely on the rhythms and the norms of their community to be able to age in place with dignity. A shiny new housing development for seniors that isn't accessible because there's no transit isn't a solution. A community where an elder can't get the food, cleaning supplies, or emotional care that they are used to is a dire feminist future. And this assumes that they don't join the growing numbers of homeless people who are older, disabled, or otherwise marginalized because of both their age and who they are.

As homelessness rates rise, the simple truth is that we have more empty housing than we need, but a side effect of gentrification is that many of the same people willing to wield police as a weapon to protect their boutique lifestyle balk at the need for services required in communities most likely to include homeless people. We know that the ranks of the homeless include elders priced out of their homes, mentally ill people, and disabled people. We know that accessible housing is expensive and difficult to access for those with minimal resources. Yet as we talk about housing instability, we tend to see it as an issue for other people to solve. But women face a wealth gap that puts them at the highest risk of being evicted, of struggling to get or stay housed. Housing is ultimately one of the most pressing feminist issues because the impact of housing instability can reverberate throughout not just one person's life but the lives of those around them.

This does not mean that feminists need to ride in as saviors. These issues are complex and require not just a great deal of knowledge, but a balancing act of existing resources and lobbying for better policy alongside the cultural work of changing the attitude that housing is not a human right. That means listening to activists and organizers, pushing politicians away from the cliff of closing public housing and toward welcoming mixed-race, mixed-income areas as the norm. It means understanding that housing is a crisis in urban, suburban, and rural areas and that the policies for one are not the policies for all. It means taking the approach that feminism can't afford to leave any woman behind—not cis, trans, disabled, poor, sex worker, you name it—and their housing has to be treated as a priority by every organization that advocates for the rights of women.

It means that feminist candidates for public office have to commit not just to doing the popular thing and supporting the middle class but also to rolling out measures to combat homelessness, from pledging to increase spending on low-cost housing to requiring developers to provide more than a token handful of units in luxury developments. It means creating meaningful plans to control rent and to revitalize areas without displacing long-term residents. It means bolstering new-age solutions for new-age problems that allow for care at home, aging in place, and a dozen other programs that provide assistance for the women who may never earn a middle-class income, but who deserve the same level of care and concern from the candidates and the systems that rely on their votes and their labor.

REPRODUCTIVE JUSTICE, EUGENICS, AND MATERNAL MORTALITY

My brush with maternal mortality came during my fifth pregnancy. Pregnancy has always been hard for me, and I have had more miscarriages than live births. I have been pregnant five times; three of those ended in miscarriages. My fifth pregnancy turned out to be my last. It was troubled from the start: I didn't experience any of the normal indicators of pregnancy—no missed periods, and in fact I was seeing an ob-gyn who specialized in treating fibroids and endometriosis in part because of the increased heaviness of my cycle—so I found out about the pregnancy when I was already ten weeks along. When my husband and I heard the news (on account of that standard pregnancy test before surgery, which turned out to be necessary after all), we talked about it, and we debated aborting—I even got as far as the clinic—before we ultimately decided that we would try to make it work. We already had two sons, and while we weren't sure we could afford a third child at that precise moment, we wanted a daughter. My doctor advised me right off the bat that she wasn't certain of a good outcome. I had large fibroids along with endometriosis, and my pregnancy would be very high risk. I did exactly what she said in terms of taking it easy, because I wanted to give that child the best possible chance. But after another eight weeks, the intermittent bleeding wouldn't stop, and I knew that there was a high chance that I would not be able to carry the pregnancy to term.

I was taking an afternoon nap when the hemorrhaging started. Waking up to find blood gushing up my body is an experience I wouldn't wish on anyone. The placental abruption that my doctor had listed as a possibility was happening, and I was going to have to do my best to take care of both of us. My husband was at work and my almost-two-year-old couldn't dial 911 for me, so I had to make it to the phone and make my own arrangements. I'll spare you the gory details of my personal splatter flick, but by the time I got to the hospital, I needed the abortion that would save my life. I didn't get it immediately, despite the bleeding, and my attempts to tell the story of how flawed my care from the first doctor was led to a piece on *Salon* and months of harassment from so-called pro-lifers, including a group that follows Jill Stanek, a former nurse best known for claiming that premature babies were being left to die in a utility closet at a hospital in Oak Lawn, Illinois.

Her followers and others sent me death threats, claimed that I had no business being pregnant because of my status as a disabled vet (I never did figure out how my bum leg and my uterus are supposed to be connected), and generally did their best to make my life hell. Some even contacted my former employer in an effort to get me fired from a job I had already left. It was harrowing, and I did my best to stand up to it while still protecting my family. Meanwhile plenty of people who had not been in my shoes were opining on what I should have done, or whether I was telling the world enough of my personal medical details, and whether I was coping the right way, as though there's a guidebook for the worst moments of your life.

I would like to be able to say that I felt supported by feminists. But it wasn't my experience. Although mainstream feminists paid lip service to the idea that I deserved support, they mostly made demands. They wanted me to speak at rallies, to testify, to give them copies of my medical records. My article had gone viral, you see, and there was no shortage of attention, though the negative reactions far outweighed the positive. Amid the lawyers and activists reaching out, no one seemed to care that I was scared, that my family was being threatened, or that I couldn't expect the same support from the police that they took for granted. I was supported by the hood. By the people who put my safety and sanity above whether I was a candidate to testify before Congress. The fact that the right to have an abortion is seen as innately feminist is accurate. But what gets obscured is that consistent access to quality health care is something everyone needs at every stage of their life. And that for many, when things go awry, the first step isn't a lawsuit; it is survival.

. . .

RECENTLY, THE FACT that the United States has a higher-than-average maternal mortality rate has brought more attention to the way racism impacts health care. We know that Black mothers in the United States die at three to four times the rate of white mothers, one of the widest racial disparities in women's health, and that personal wealth does not protect Black mothers from that higher risk. Serena Williams's story of having to demand necessary health care to prevent a pulmonary embolism or worse is a prime example. She's wealthy and highly visible; the same is true of her husband. She's well versed in her own health-care needs, and she still had to argue with the staff to get the necessary treatment.

However, while abortion is seen as a feminist issue, access to health care is not necessarily framed that way. Reproductive justice needs to be reframed to include the entire spectrum of choices surrounding every stage of women's health, reproductive and otherwise. The United States is constantly facing a health-care crisis, and only some people seem to understand that the issues are related and reflect a systemic failure.

Some forty-five thousand people were dying each year from a lack of insurance before the Affordable Care Act. And that's just from a lack of insurance. Add to that the people who die as a result of reaching lifetime maximums for care, or from unapproved treatments, and the number climbs. Now, as we talk about the disparity in maternal mortality rates by race, there has to be a shift in how we approach health-care access. It has to be seen as a right, not as a commodity or an option. And health-care providers have to interrogate what biases they have brought into the ways they approach patient care.

Persistent racist beliefs in medicine and otherwise are at the root of ongoing racial disparities in treatment and patient out-comes; this represents a challenge not only for twenty-first-century medical providers, but for those who fight for the access of marginalized communities to quality health care. Problems are amplified by unconscious biases that are embedded in the medical system, affecting quality of care in stark and subtle ways ranging from experiences like mine, where the pregnancy was not viable but there was plenty of judgment about what I should have done, to situations where motherhood is a death sentence because no one gets it together in time.

This is an issue that spans communities with Black, Latina, and Indigenous women facing similar complications as a result of bigotry. Alongside "Mississippi appendectomies" (which was another name for unnecessary hysterectomies performed at teach-ing hospitals in the South on Black women), there was the forced sterilization of Indigenous Americans, which persisted into the 1970s and '80s, with young women receiving tubal liga-tions when they were ostensibly getting appendectomies. Ulti-mately an estimated 25 to 50 percent of Indigenous women were sterilized between 1970 and 1976. Forced sterilization programs are also a part of history in Puerto Rico, where sterilization rates are said to be among the highest in the world. Most recently, California prisons were alleged to have authorized coerced ster-ilization of nearly 150 female inmates between 2006 and 2010.

In countries where eugenics by way of coerced sterilization is not just a shameful history but sometimes still a current issue, we have to interrogate the lack of quality care available to the populations most impacted by eugenics. Driven by prejudiced notions, these programs informed policies on immigration and segregation, and now seem to be impacting maternal health care.

In a climate where society doesn't value families of color, is it any wonder that the right to have children at all is still contested? Reproductive justice rightfully focuses on preserving the right to choose, but too often advocates center on access to contraception at the expense of communities that are still facing other obstacles. True reproductive justice involves not only access to affordable birth control, abortion, and health care but also providing access to those who are imprisoned, who are in immigration detention centers, who are seen as unworthy of controlling their own lives for a variety of reasons. And that's before we get into the ways that trans, nonbinary, and intersex people are impacted by a framework that largely prioritizes the needs of cis white middle-class women.

Reproductive health care is about bodily autonomy, which is something trans people are often denied because of transphobia. Aside from being assigned a gender at birth that may not match their identity, they face obstacles in accessing medical care in general. Trans people can face ignorance or outright prejudice from medical professionals, who then become yet another barrier to quality care. Everything from accessing basic health care to safe hormone regimens can be difficult or even impossible depending on location and finances. Sadly, when some care providers discovered that their patients were trans people, their discriminatory attitudes increased to the point of refusing to write prescriptions or sometimes even see trans patients again. Others claimed they didn't understand the needs of the transgender community, but also refused to seek out the education they lacked. That leaves trans patients in the awkward position of paying out of pocket for appointments they'll spend providing free education to health-care providers.

A dear friend who transitioned outside the United States got breast cancer some years ago. Her care should have been fairly straightforward; she makes a good living, has excellent insurance, and lives in a state that has long had protections for LGBTQIA people codified in the law. But her excellent insurance routed her to a specialist who, while not outright discriminatory, had very little information about the transition process. So for a part of almost every appointment with her oncologist, my friend had to answer invasive questions that had nothing to do with her medical care. She wanted to be healed, needed this doctor's help, and felt pressured into maintaining a cordial relationship while her doctor processed his feelings about gender in the midst of her treatment. It was incredibly unprofessional, and anytime she attempted to redirect the conversation he was quick to assert that he just wanted to be a better doctor. His prurient curiosity about how her wife had handled her transition mattered more to him than professional ethics. And yet, she was able to get the treatment she needed; she had to count that as a win.

With the recent proposal from the Trump administration to

roll back protections that prevent doctors from legally discriminating based on gender identity, the American government stands ready to not only allow doctors to refuse to treat trans patients, but to actively encourage this discrimination. That can mean someone who is gender nonconforming could go to the doctor for a persistent cough, and instead of their lung function being evaluated they could be turned away with no legal recourse. It won't matter if the cough is bronchitis, tuberculosis, or lung cancer, because unless they can find a series of good doctors, their health is going to be compromised.

While being educated about your own health can lead to better care outcomes, this goes beyond advocacy and into an exploitation of a marginalized community as a walking unpaid resource. Because of bigotry, providers who refuse to see trans patients contribute to a medical culture where people who already have difficulty obtaining providers can't easily seek out those who are better versed in their care. That means trans patients can be forced to repeatedly engage with situations that can trigger dysphoria in order to access any level of care.

And gender dysphoria can be fatal if untreated: a staggering 41 percent of the trans community has attempted suicide. Trauma in reproductive health services can drive trans people into fearing the health-care system as a whole. Between discrimination and the fear that keeps marginalized people out of doctors' offices, trans people are less likely to get preventive care and more likely to develop complications from delayed care. This can include care during an abortion or during pregnancy. For nonbinary and trans people, access to reproductive care is already fraught because of limited access due to the economic and social barriers. Add in any health-care trauma, and the very place you should be able to get help becomes yet another emotional minefield.

It's also critical to discuss the fact that a common reason given for a need to keep abortion accessible is fetal disability. On the one hand, no one should be forced to have a child they do not want; on the other, even though feminism as a movement is committed to eliminating discrimination, a central tenet of the right to choose should not hinge on discriminatory logic. Arguments that disability is a reason abortion needs to be legal frame being disabled as a condition incompatible with a healthy, fulfilling life. You can argue for the right to choose without arguing against the right of people with disabilities to exist.

Disability should not be a death sentence. Does that mean the right to choose should be abrogated? No. I firmly believe that abortion should be the decision of the pregnant person. But much of the concern around abortion rates has centered on the idea that abortion on demand is eugenics in action. Reproductive justice advocates should never parrot the rhetoric of eugenicists, especially around the idea that only some people are fit to exist.

Reproductive justice is fundamentally about agency and autonomy. Abortion rights should never be a fight over the value of disabled lives, because disabled people absolutely deserve to exist. Fetuses, who are potential life with no capability of surviving on their own, and are not the same as humans living on their own outside the womb, should be framed in conversations as exactly that.

Higher abortion rates in low-income communities are sometimes connected by anti-choice groups to eugenics as well. Because of environmental racism, limited access to prenatal care,
and subpar nutrition and housing for many in marginalized
communities, the risk factors for having a child with a serious
disability are higher than average. Add in the fact that resources
are limited not only for children with disabilities but also for
adults with disabilities, and those higher rates of pregnancy ter-
mination make sense.

That lack of resources is what we should be addressing when
we talk about reproductive justice. The mainstream reproductive rights movement does not talk about disability enough to
even know how to address these concerns. Instead the pro-life
movement has successfully centered itself as the movement concerned with the right of disabled children to be born. As that
movement has seized control of this conversation, pro-choice
activists have largely absolved themselves of the responsibility
of advocating for reproductive options for disabled *adults*, and
of getting into a discussion of what it means to screen for disability as standard medical care. In a reproductive rights framework that centers on autonomy and self-determination, there
should be a clear connection with disability rights activism.

Instead, a coalition of misogynists, racists, and violent terror-
ists masquerading as people concerned with the right to life
have made more visible attempts to include people with disabilities. And they are supported by people who assert that they
truly believe in the right to life, and who may indeed mean the

words they say with no consideration for the very real consequences of supporting anti-choice rhetoric for people who are
not them. Anyone can be a hypocrite, including those who claim
to rescue children via adoption. Does that mean that everyone
who adopts a child with a disability is doing so from a cynical
place? Absolutely not.

But there are some very real problems with the way that anti-
choice groups will use children as props in their campaigns.
They bolster their arguments by adopting children with disabilities, tell purple prose–laden stories about the miraculous love
they have found by "saving" those children, and then vote for the
candidates who will remove services for disabled people from
their communities. More concerned with their public messaging than any real change, they undermine the health-care access
that might provide the best chance at an independent, fulfilling
life for people with disabilities. While fetal disability narratives
are central to pro-life rhetoric, and pro-life feminists are quick
to point to abortions of fetuses with disabilities as a form of eugenics, they falter at follow-up care and concern.

True reproductive justice advocates have done a better job
of including a disability rights framework in the broader movement, but they too have faltered at being truly inclusive of people with disabilities and their concerns. It's hard to have a
conversation across these communities when an accessibility
framework is lacking in choosing locations for meetings, meetings lack services to make them accessible for those who are
hard of hearing or deaf, or other obstacles arise because activ-

ists are too used to speaking for communities instead of listening to them.

It's uncomfortable and sometimes enraging to consider a dialogue with the pro-life movement, but without it, they will be able to continue the wholesale appropriation of a disability rights framework for a movement that ultimately betrays everyone. No one in reproductive justice should want to identify as a eugenicist, not just because it is a fake label the pro-life movement uses on people who advocate for abortion rights. They should want to avoid eugenicist rhetoric because it can ultimately only serve to undermine the work of reproductive justice.

When the pro-life movement brings up the women who abort fetuses with Down syndrome diagnoses, reproductive justice advocates need a better response than ignoring it. The conversation needs to be centered on resources, on support, and on countering ableist narratives. When they frame these statistics as proof of eugenics, as proof that the abortion rights movement doesn't care about people with disabilities, reproductive justice feminists must be ready to frame disability not just in terms of children and fetuses but also in terms of adults with disabilities. The conversation about the right to choose should explicitly include that right for people with disabilities. It has to talk about the infrastructure and the access that they might need. It has to talk about the rights of people with disabilities to control their own fertility and sexuality.

When mainstream feminists don't talk about the infrastructure that contributes to people aborting fetuses with disabilities, it leaves a ready-made space for those who would infringe on the right to choose. Like other people who have abortions, those who choose to abort fetuses with congenital abnormalities most likely do so because they already have children they're providing for, they live in poverty, and/or they experience other structural oppression that prevents them from being able to commit to caring for a child with a disability. It is important for reproductive rights and reproductive justice frameworks to recognize that the choice to carry to term or to abort is heavily influenced by class, race, and other obstacles created by marginalization. Parents with disabilities are stigmatized as being unable to appropriately care for their children no matter how many successfully raise families. Some people with disabilities are at risk of being sterilized as a result of that stigma. Others were sterilized without consent based on the idea that they would have children with disabilities and thus create an intergenerational cycle of dependency on the minimal resources available.

In general, having children is expensive, and the lack of substantial social safety in the United States makes it even more difficult for low-income parents already struggling to afford the basics of housing, childcare, and medical care. Children with disabilities may require expensive specialized health care, educational support, a specialized diet, and therapy, and reproductive justice has to address what happens after a child is born. By and large, parents can't afford to not work outside the home, which means that they must pay for childcare or attempt to cobble together some form of at-home care with opposite work schedules. There is a devastating choice on the table: a lack of family time and caregiver support or a substantial loss of income. Because institutions are not designed to help parents raise high-needs children, it becomes much easier to argue that children with disabilities are a burden to be avoided instead of addressing the paucity of resources.

Sympathy also bleeds away for parents of children with disabilities and parents with disabilities, particularly when those parents are of color, are LGBTQIA, or are anything outside the expected "traditional" middle-class, able-bodied, cis, white family dynamic. Their disability, race, immigration status, gender identity, sexual orientation, or income level becomes the center of a debate over their right to have a family instead of plans to support those families. Because like race, disability has long been an excuse for the medical establishment to forcibly sterilize people, and any concept of reproductive justice must include an understanding of that history.

And a true reproductive justice framework has to challenge the rights of guardians of people with disabilities to request, without their consent, sterilization of those who depend on them. As Human Rights Watch notes, people with disabilities who are sterilized and are unable to comprehend or consent to the procedure are particularly vulnerable to abuse.

We must be careful to avoid contributing to a damaging narrative about people with disabilities. Feminism can't parrot the idea that people with disabilities are a drain on resources and thus their lives are worth less. Instead of bolstering the eugenicist myth that people with disabilities are a burden on the community and undeserving of public funding, we must address the fact that it is so expensive for families to raise children with disabilities in a society that doesn't provide for anyone's needs adequately. We must push back against the idea that disability status is a predictor of fitness to exist, to be heard, to have a choice. Eugenics makes the argument that members of many communities are not worthy or capable of making their own reproductive choices, and thus are not fit to be parents. That rhetoric is carried from pop culture all the way through to medical science.

THOUGH THE PRIMARY FOCUS of maternal mortality research has been on Black mothers in the United States because the rates of maternal mortality are highest for us (Black women are 243 percent more likely to die from pregnancy-related causes), the same factors rear their heads in many communities. The outcomes in those communities, however, are slightly better, because there's less of a stake in the idea that they don't deserve respect or care. For Black communities in the United States, even when factors such as physical health, access to prenatal care, income level, education, and socioeconomic status are controlled for, Black women are still far more likely to experience maternal mortality at rates that hark back to the days when Black motherhood was seen as a problem to be solved with sterilization.

Social and environmental risk factors that influence poor maternal health outcomes disproportionately impact marginalized communities. Poverty-based risk factors, from housing instability to increased exposure to toxins because of subpar housing to increased exposure to violence, contribute to higher stress levels and lower access to quality health care, including comprehensive mental health services. Additional factors like workplace barriers and food insecurity can easily trap someone in a toxic environment and pregnancy in the United States.

In that same vein, we must be willing to confront the *-isms* that let people think maternity is only something to celebrate when the mother is white. If you read comments on articles about Black moms like Serena Williams, Beyoncé, or Meghan Markle, you notice a theme in the racism. A Black mom is somehow gross for cradling her pregnant belly, but the same posters find it adorable when white women do it. It's a passive form of racism, rarely examined, much less discussed. And yeah, comments are a cesspool, but medical staff make comments on forums too. So when you see people on Twitter, Instagram, or Facebook claim the babies of Black moms are meal tickets or monkeys, or when they make hate into a hobby so thoroughly that they are profiled for it in the press, you have to ask yourself if they're the kind of medical professional who treats babies like puppets and calls them Satan for Snapchat points.

When someone like Serena Williams or Beyoncé Knowles-Carter shares her stories of pregnancy complications and concerns, it briefly pushes the problem of the maternal deaths of Black women front and center in mainstream feminist media. But it shouldn't take an impassioned story from one of the most famous Black women in the world to get it into everyone's head that America can no longer ignore the health of Black mothers.

Fully addressing the issue requires interrogation of not only the obvious flaws within the medical system but also all the other institutions that can affect various aspects of health-care access and quality for marginalized people. For too long, the same systems and institutions that oversaw slavery, Indian boarding schools, and eugenics programs have been allowed to operate without dealing with the biases rooted in their formation. Fully addressing maternal mortality calls for an acknowledgment that unexamined biases within the medical system and outside have been a key factor in the paucity of care for those communities where motherhood is perceived as a sin instead of a sacrament.

Imagery of white motherhood is standard in media, complete with the seemingly de rigueur write-ups from white feminists about the ways becoming a mother has changed their lives. Often hidden in those pieces is something casual about the caregivers they hire to help out. If you look closely, you can see the telltale marks of people who need to rely on communities of color for labor but who don't really engage with what that means in any meaningful way. In a way, that reaction is bolstered by the world around us: we see white moms on TV, on billboards, on posters, and more. No matter if the story is sextuplets or a family of nineteen, TV channels are happy to take us inside the lives of those families. To humanize and validate and valorize their choices. Yet despite a history of Black, Asian, Indigenous, and Latinx caregivers for the white children of those families, popular media would have you believe that every other group is unqualified to care for or raise their own children.

Mothers and children who are not white have long been devalued in American society. Entire Indigenous families were massacred to create what we now think of as America. During slavery, Black women were treated as chattel, their offspring human capital to fund the building of white wealth. The romanticized image of the plantation hinges on the idea that Black parents lacked the emotional capacity to care for their children. That mythos persists today in Welfare Queen narratives that position children as checks and not as much-loved and wanted parts of a family. Whether the slur is "anchor babies" or something else, no one is safe from the racist lie that only white parents have the emotional capacity to actually want their children.

Indeed, despite the fact that assaults on marginalized bodies and their reproductive freedom have been well documented, mainstream feminist narratives often fail to engage with the consequences of that messaging on the culture or on the policies that come about in the wake of these constructs.

And while the most overt trappings of subjugation are no longer present in the public eye in America, the remnants can be seen throughout the very systems meant to be counteracting bigotry in the present day. Marginalized families have been torn apart due to state violence, whether that be mass incarceration or the impact of punitive policies toward the poor. Incarcerated women are still being sterilized without their consent; access to health care for migrant workers is impacted by public policy that punishes them for seeking help; those in low-paying jobs struggle not only to access care, but to be treated well once they receive it.

Stereotypical images and perceptions of marginalized people within the media aren't just the province of conservative policy makers—even the way abortion access is discussed for low-income communities is framed in a manner that invokes sexual promiscuity and irresponsibility as reasons that access is needed. Only recently have we seen the idea espoused in the mainstream that poor people deserve to choose their family size. Far too often the need to limit family size is presented as a solution for resource issues that devalues those families and causes society to view them as less worthy to exist. The ripple effects of this attitude can be seen in how mainstream feminist organizations often neglect to respond to policies and programs that show minimal regard for the health of marginalized communities. The devaluation of families of color is manifested through the unchallenged structural racism of a system wherein public policies, institutional practices, and media representations not only work together to create the significant Black-white gap in maternal mortality but also contribute to the erasure of the maternal mortality rates in other marginalized communities.

Organizations led by marginalized communities are working to fix the problem, but challenging white supremacy in these spaces can't just be the work of those most impacted. By confronting the role that racism plays in reproductive health spaces, feminism can help to reduce maternal mortality and in turn change the future for many communities.

Feminist programs that work toward increasing access to quality health care, along with addressing racial bias among health-care providers, can address important aspects of a comprehensive approach to reducing maternal mortality. Bolstering efforts to block proposals to strip maternity care from the list of essential health benefits is a great step. But so is protecting Medicaid, and challenging attempts to impose work requirements as a condition for health-care coverage through the program.

Reproductive justice means not just fighting to defend Planned Parenthood or the Title X family planning program. It also means protecting nutrition programs such as the Women, Infants, and Children (WIC) program and the Supplemental Nutrition Assistance Program (SNAP). As politicians rush to show their disregard for low-income people struggling to feed their families, feminism has to step up and support the work of advocates for all communities. For those already dealing with so many obstacles within their communities, it's harder to find the energy to also fight for higher-quality care without support from those with more resources.

PARENTING WHILE MARGINALIZED

When I was eight years old, my uncle got drunk, showed up at my grandparents' house, and waved a gun around for a couple of hours while making threats. It was some dispute over money that no one can really remember now, but what I do remember is that he wasn't afraid to do it because he knew my grandfather wasn't home. His wife (the aunt with whom he was having the money issues) didn't live there, but he knew she had guns in her house. And since she had already responded to his earlier outbursts of violence by stabbing him or shooting at him, he knew better than to try her.

He thought that a houseful of women was an easy target as long as my grandfather wasn't home. He was wrong. My aunt who did live there was more than willing to fend him off with her courage and a bottle ready to go upside his head. What I remember most about that night isn't the gun or the drunken ranting. It's that after he left, she sat down to do her homework and I sat down with her to do mine. I wasn't her child, but she was co-parenting me with my grandparents, and there was work to be done. She made sure I had a clear idea of what I needed to do so that I might have a future without the kind of instability that had marked my life so far.

I joined the army after high school without much thought beyond the promised narratives about opportunity. Meeting my first husband and having my first child were steps in the road of my life that had very little to do with any ideas about tradition. I got married so we could be stationed in the same place, got pregnant because we decided we wanted kids. When I thought about having a child, I thought in terms of the life I wanted for my family. I never wanted my children to have to worry about drunk men, much less drunk men with guns.

Because of nights like that, I never really participated in the Mommy Wars. Life had taught me early and often that having food was far more important than fussing over whether it was from the right places. A safe, stable home was what mattered, not whether that home was in the right zip code. Before my oldest son's little eyes could even focus, I found myself dealing with other people's assumptions about whether I was qualified to make decisions for him because I was poor and Black.

I wasn't a single mother, but doctors would act like I was, unless my then-husband was physically in the room. Sometimes even though we were very clear that I was the one staying home with our baby, they would start talking to him like he was the one qualified to make decisions because he was white. The hilarious and depressing thing is that these were often white women who were ostensibly feminist. They had somehow convinced themselves that my socioeconomic status meant that what I needed most was their input on parenting as though their "benevolent" racist assumptions had any value in my life.

A conversation about something as mundane as how I burped him (he preferred to lie across a knee) turned into a condescending lecture on the "right way" to burp from a white administrator. One of the Latinx nurses interjected to say that the way I was doing it was fine, but the white admin was oddly insistent that it was wrong. Baby-faced and Black added up in her head to mean I needed someone to teach me how to burp a child I'd carried and would be raising to adulthood. Later when he was in preschool, his allergy to milk was questioned by the preschool director. Not because he lacked a doctor's note, but because she thought asking a friend who was a nutritionist was the same as me taking him to see his pediatrician. She decided to change his diet based on her assumptions, not on his needs, and was deeply offended when I didn't welcome her help. Yet the dietary changes she attempted to make nearly landed him in the ER.

Getting through breast-feeding versus formula and when to vaccinate was the easiest part of learning how to be a good parent. The hard part was having to admit to myself that as far as other people were concerned, their own racist assumptions trumped all of my efforts to keep my family on track even as the obstacles ranged from the mundane to the major. I had to deal with leaving a bad marriage with no money, going to college with a child, and creating a path for us to move forward.

In the Mommy Wars version of parenting, my inability to provide an organic diet might mean I didn't care enough. In reality the occasional pack of Oreos meant he could have almond milk and fresh veggies while I lived on a diet of caffeine and cheap fast food. Moving out of my apartment and into public housing might have looked like a failure from the outside. But from the inside it meant that I could eat regular meals too. Years of having to make hard choices without good choices taught me some lessons about what kind of parenting issues really matter.

As my sons have matured, my concerns have been less about the kinds of things that seem to be held up as the first priority by outsiders. Like most Black parents, I have to teach my sons about race and how it will impact the way people perceive them. We don't spend a lot of time stressing about whether their school has the right playground materials. Instead, we're concerned with whether their school is going to survive the latest round of closures and stay open. Whether the teachers are getting paid, and of course, whether there are police officers in their building. It's not a question of helicopter parenting or bulldozer parenting; it's survival parenting.

For parents in marginalized communities, it's keeping kids out of gangs, out of the crossfire, and out of jail that are paramount concerns. For some communities it is avoiding deportation of the parents or of the children. There's no thought of being able to direct every aspect of their life or of clearing the way for things to be easy for them. You're prepping them for a life where they will need to be resourceful, resilient, and still able to dream.

We know that sexism is a problem, we know that misogyny is a problem, but we don't always want to address the way racism plays a role in how those things can manifest between groups of women. In a country with a massive wealth gap that is directly tied to race, what does it mean to frame good parenting as making choices that are only accessible for those with excess income? What does it mean to assume that to be poor and not white means you are less capable of being a good parent? Especially when you factor in the power that white women can have over women of color and their children.

Insisting it is harmless fun to pander to racist stereotypes or feigning a complete lack of knowledge about why parents of color are concerned about obstacles that are specific to their communities requires a level of shortsightedness that is intrinsically dangerous to all children. We didn't create child labor laws simply because we thought it was a good idea; we did it because kids need to be protected in ways adults don't. For marginalized parents, every decision carries the additional risk of their children being impacted by someone else's bias.

The fear of losing your child because of problems like chronic tardiness, because you chose to use a friend's address to get them into a better school, or because you had to work and didn't have childcare is ever present. Yet you can't let that fear dictate your decisions. Not if you want to keep your child fed and clothed and housed. Being a marginalized parent is an emotional and social tightrope over a hard floor without a net.

I don't pretend to know what it would be like to raise a child on a reservation, or to be a migrant worker who has to worry about deportation and access to education. I do know that I need to listen to the women in those positions, follow their lead on what would help the most and what would be detrimental. They are the experts in their own needs, and I can recognize that those needs being different doesn't make them less important.

More people are talking about police brutality. Unfortunately, it is often framed solely as a racial issue, one that disproportionately impacts Black men, erasing its impact on young Black women. Or on those who are trans or genderqueer. Or on other communities of color that are not Black. Different risk factors aren't the same as no risk factors. We don't talk about over-policing or police brutality as feminist issues, yet for women of color, policing can be a major source of structural oppression. In fact, the second most common complaint against police officers is sexual misconduct. That doesn't start at adulthood. Teenagers are at risk, often in the very places that should be safe, because the default assumption is that adding more cops will fix the problem.

We know fewer names of Black women, cis and trans, who have been victims of police brutality than we do any other group. There is little discussion about their risk of sexual assault, arrest, and even death. The fact that fewer cis Black women die from police brutality supports the erroneous idea that to be a Black woman is to be safer from oppression than a Black man. By the same token, erasing the ways that police misconduct can be sexual by framing it as only being about physical violence contributes to the risks faced by women in marginalized communities. It also ignores that for young people, the risk of being exploited by authority figures is higher. It isn't just children of color at risk; ignoring police brutality and misconduct puts all but the most privileged and insulated children at risk.

The grace you show to white kids? Try showing it to all kids. Our girls aren't grown at five and our boys aren't weapons at birth. I can tell stories of being harassed by cops, of dealing with predatory adults through puberty, and they are all hard to tell and harder to hear. But if they only make *me* human to you, and not the rest of my community, not other communities, then what good is your feminism? What good are the clucking and the head shaking that don't challenge the racist paradigms in place?

So why aren't we talking about parenting while marginalized as a feminist issue? Why aren't we looking at parenting less as a competition and more as an aspect of our society that needs serious intervention directly with white women and racial bias? The awkward reality of the school-to-prison pipeline is that Black youth are most at risk from the conscious and unconscious biases playing into the decision of involving police in school discipline. Teaching is a profession that is predominantly white and female. How do you discuss over-policing and discrimination as a feminist issue when women who fit the mainstream idea of feminism are most likely to be complicit in a particular form of oppression?

The answer, of course, is to confront the problem—for feminism to examine the biases that contribute to school administrators seeing a white girl's vandalism as a prank resolved with restitution, and a Black girl's vandalism as a crime requiring judicial intervention. Yes, it is important for women to work together against gender oppression. But which women? Which forms of gender oppression? After all, cis women can and do oppress trans women, white women have the institutional and social power to oppress women of color, able-bodied women can oppress people with disabilities, and so on. Oppression of women isn't just an external force; it happens between groups of women as well. While the oppressed can and do fight oppression, what happens when the people who are supposed to be your allies on one axis are your oppressors on another?

If you are a school-aged Black kid, and unexamined internalized racism makes your teacher perceive you as a threat when you act out in the same way as a white classmate who will be seen as troubled and in need of counseling, what is your recourse? What happens when your empowerment is a threat to the status quo? If you don't fit in as one of the "good kids" because of your skin color and your hair texture, how do you become a part of the community? None of these questions have easy answers, but it is not up to the kids to come up with the answers. Nor, to be honest, is it the duty of adult Black women to convince white feminists of their humanity or the right of their children to exist and have access to the same opportunities as anyone else.

Mainstream white feminists will have to confront the racism of white women and the harm it does, without passing the buck to white men. Whether it is the way that white women in schools can wield institutional power against youths of color, or the message sent in New York when teachers in Staten Island wear shirts to support the police officer who killed Eric Garner, the conversation is long overdue. Calls for solidarity or sisterhood have to begin with the idea that all women matter, that all families matter, that issues around caring for children don't just come down to who is doing more work inside the home, but also to how children are being treated by society. If the idea that a Black girl could be innocent enough to do the wrong thing and still deserve a future is anathema to you, then you don't belong in a classroom, and you don't belong in the feminist movement either. Not until you can look at little Black girls and envision the same possibilities you do for little white girls.

And that isn't a responsibility that stops with Black girls. Every girl of every race deserves access to opportunity, deserves to have her culture and community respected. For non-Black parents of color, the issues may be slightly different, but the underlying impact is often the same. When a presidential candidate seriously intimates that Mexican immigrants are rapists, and a white feminist comedian makes jokes along those same lines, what's the difference in social impact? Yes, that candidate might promise to make a bunch of laws and build a wall, but the one who makes it sound less racist is the white feminist who normalizes that kind of rhetoric by undermining the seriousness of the racism inherent in it.

Fear of a Black man, boy, or genderqueer teen simply for existing isn't about actual threat; it's about the internalized racism and anti-Blackness that permeates our culture, and making light of that dangerous ideology normalizes the violence against marginalized communities.

After all, one of the things Black children have in common with Indigenous and migrant children is a higher-than-normal risk of being taken into foster care. We skirt around the edges of the issues that poverty creates for parents who don't have the protection of privilege. Yes, the state stepping in to address issues of abuse or neglect is absolutely one that I support. But the most common narrative around is a white savior narrative, which feeds the idea that a child of color is intrinsically better off with a wealthy parent, even if that parent doesn't share their ethnic or racial background. We assume that a lack of financial stability is an indicator of parental ability, despite knowing that the reasons for the wealth gap have very little to do with what might be best for a child emotionally and socially.

The crushing reality of poverty can force parents to make choices that put children at risk, such as leaving them home alone or with unsafe caregivers. Toxic stress can leave parents too numb to meet the emotional needs of their children. This matters a great deal because most of the children removed from their homes are taken because of neglect, not abuse. Poverty can look like neglect, even if a parent is doing their very best. When your income is substantially below what you need to raise your child, and every possible economic solution is unavailable, ineffective, or illegal, then what do you do?

When your child's care costs more than you make an hour and subsidy programs are underfunded or nonexistent, but you have to work because of public aid requirements to be able to access TANF, food stamps, and so on, then you cobble together what you can when you can, but you don't have a good choice to make. You just have to make the best of your situation and hope you don't run afoul of the law. This is especially difficult now in the era of the helicopter parent. Financially well-off, socially privileged, and almost completely ignorant of the lifestyles of those with less, they are among the most likely to call the authorities over perceived neglect as mundane as a child walking home alone.

Of course, you can argue that they are only trying to act in the child's best interests, but if the child's best interests are the only concern, then alleviating poverty for low-income parents would be a primary feminist issue. Instead, we find mainstream feminism hunkered down in the Hipster Mommy Wars, where at best the discussion is about the guilt you might feel for leaving your child with a nanny while you go to work. A long, navelgazing paragraph about the guilt you might feel for being not feminist enough because you choose to stay home might be personally satisfying, but what does it do for marginalized parents?

Educating yourself on the issues that others are facing is perhaps the easiest way for a feminist to address parenting. I didn't learn about Indigenous children and foster care by accident; I actively sought out more information on the Indian Child Welfare Act after a string of court cases were covered in the news. Does that mean I am an expert on ICWA? Of course not, but understanding the awful legacy of boarding schools for Indigenous Americans helped me grasp the importance of it—and thus the importance of listening to the activists who fight so hard to keep children in their community even when family situations are imperfect. It's easy to say that "only love matters" when you assume that a culture has no value, and that erasing a child's connection to it isn't damaging.

Internalized bias may make it easier to believe in racist myths that dehumanize parents from severely disadvantaged communities, but the onus is on those with privilege, as feminists and as parents, to check themselves, to ask what they might be willing to do in order to give their children access to a life they never had. Would they also risk life and limb to immigrate regardless of arbitrary borders and laws? Would they sell drugs? Privilege, especially economic privilege, can make it easy to forget that while every parent faces challenges, not every parent has the same resources.

These days my oldest child is in college at my alma mater. My youngest is in middle school. I could pretend that being middle class–adjacent now means that I have forgotten where I came from, forgotten what it took to get me from "at-risk youth" to a published writer with two degrees. But that wouldn't serve my community, wouldn't be a good example to my children, and wouldn't let me live with myself. This veneer of respectability that came from getting more education and being able to write professionally is nice. I like knowing that people will listen to what I have to say, but I'm always aware that people don't usually listen to the Black girls like me, and that even now some will carve out a space for me that is separate from the other people like me. Because you'll decide that me being able to get where they didn't means they aren't trying hard enough. In fact they're trying just as hard, but they didn't have the same luck, the same relatives, the same community. It's not a question of "Why can't they do what you did?" It's a question of "Why can't we give everyone else the same support and access?" That's the battle feminism should be fighting. Without the extra obstacles of racism and classism, so many more people like me would be succeeding. That's the future this liberal wants to live in.

ALLIES, ANGER, AND ACCOMPLICES

I used to be terrible about some trans and gender-nonconforming issues, specifically around bathrooms. It wasn't in my mind a big deal to have separate bathrooms. Then a friend pointed out that not being able to use the bathroom in public is tantamount to being forced out of normal, everyday life. I had been a good self-identified ally to trans and nonbinary people, never once thinking that they didn't have the right to exist or wanting them to be isolated or excluded from success in the workplace.

I didn't have a problem with trans women in the ladies' room and I thought that was enough. I didn't have to worry about a bathroom that matched my gender identity being available, so it never occurred to me how difficult or dangerous it might be for someone who isn't cisgender. But I hadn't been a good accomplice. Being an ally is just the first step, the simplest one. It is the space wherein the privileged begin to accept the flawed dynamics that make for inequality. Being a good ally isn't easy, isn't something you can leap into, though it can feel like you're suddenly a know-it-all superhero. Privilege not only blinds you to oppression, it blinds you to your own ignorance even when you notice the oppression.

Why is becoming an ally so hard? Many would-be allies have an immediate reaction of defensiveness when someone challenges them on their advice, their intentions, their need to be centered. It's in that precise moment that they need to stop, step back, and realize they are still part of the problem. It is never the privileged outsider who gets to decide when they're a good ally. Especially not if they want to use their status as an ally to excuse whatever they have done that has offended someone in the group they claim to be supporting.

A common problem is that when allies are challenged, they often insist that there is no way they could be part of the problem. They default to rattling off an extensive résumé of what they've "done for you people." Instead of listening to the concerns a marginalized person is trying to express, they whip out the "I Marched with Dr. King, I Was an Ally When No One Else Was, I Earned the Right to Say These Things in the Past" laundry list, which often is intended to cover everything without ever engaging with the current problem. It's difficult to stand outside the mind-set that privilege creates, to let go of "those people" narratives that position the privileged as an authority on the experiences of others.

Identifying yourself as an ally is a convenient way to give yourself a pass for dismissing the words or experiences of people with less privilege and power than you. You can be in their corner, right up until it makes you feel uncomfortable. Then because you think they're overreacting or that it has "nothing to do with race," you can tell yourself that you tried to help, that "those people" are really the problem. If you stop being an ally or never manage to become a good ally, you can assuage any possible guilt by coddling yourself with fond memories of that one time you did something. It doesn't even matter if it was what was needed, as long as it makes you feel better.

Allies tend to crowd out the space for anger with their demands that things be comfortable for them. They want to be educated, want someone to be kind to them whether they have earned that kindness or not. The process of becoming an ally requires a lot of emotional investment, and far too often the heavy lifting of that emotional labor is done by the marginalized, not by the privileged. But part of the journey from being a would-be ally to becoming an ally to actually being an accomplice is anger.

Anger doesn't have to be erudite to be valid. It doesn't have to be nice or calm in order to be heard. In fact, I would argue that despite narratives that present the anger of Black women as dangerous, that render being angry in public a reason to tune out the voices of marginalized people, it is that anger and the expressing of it that saves communities. No one has ever freed themselves from oppression by asking nicely. Instead they had to fight, sometimes with words and sometimes with bullets. I come from people who only asked once, then, well, they got down to the business of taking what society refused to give them—respect, peace, rights, you name it—and the movements to achieve it have been derided as rude. Too loud, too angry, too much. But they were effective, and ultimately laid the groundwork for anger to be seen as something we might not always need.

Anger can be cathartic, motivating, and above all else an expression of the innate humanity of any community. Demands that the oppressed be calm and polite and that forgiveness come before all else are fundamentally dehumanizing. If your child is killed by police, if the water in your community is poisoned, if a mockery is made of your grief, how do you feel? Do you want to be calm and quiet? Do you want to forgive in order to make everyone else comfortable? Or do you want to scream, to yell, to demand justice for the wrongs done?

Anger gets the petitions out, it motivates marches, it gets people to the ballot. Anger is sometimes the only fuel left at the end of a long, horrible day, week, month, or generation. It's a powerful force, and sometimes when oppressors want to demonize the oppressed, the first thing they point to is anger. "Why must you be so mean?" or "I'm trying to help."

There's an element of saviorism that creeps into identifying as an ally. On paper being an ally sounds great: you come in and you use your privilege to help a marginalized person or group. But when we talk about an intersectional approach to feminism, we also have to understand that the reason the concept of intersectionality centers on Black women and justice is that Black women are the least likely to have the kind of class privilege that can grant them access to anything like justice. Even now, with camera phones and body cams to document wrongdoing, being able to generate public support can make a huge difference in whether justice is even an option.

After all the hashtags and the arguments online and off, I am perhaps best known for my anger, the way I wield it, and the way it has been framed as too dangerous. My rage is sometimes eloquent and often effective, and it occasionally feels eviscerating in its intensity. I believe in rage, believe in aiming it when I unleash it because I know it can be so powerful. My targets tend to be up, not down or sideways, from where I sit.

It's true that social media has made it easier to see inflamed emotions. Facebook and Twitter are places where the marginalized can't be silenced as easily. It's a place where attracting attention to social ills is easier if solutions aren't necessarily forthcoming. On social media, the narratives around anger, especially public anger, can be skewed by the collision of different social norms. But to paraphrase James Baldwin, to be aware of what is happening in this world is to be in an almost perpetual state of rage. Everyone should be angry about injustice, not just those experiencing it.

And we can't afford to shy away from anger. Because the bigots who use anger as a political tool, as a way to motivate, as an incitement to violence, also have access to large platforms. And in some ways, they have the upper hand in terms of organizing oppression precisely because any attempts to confront issues within feminism are met by calls to not be divisive, at the expense of being effective and honest. While white male politicians and pundits are some of the biggest peddlers of rage, the fact is that misogyny and racism creep into interpretations of rage from the marginalized. The power that could be brought to bear by addressing the roots of anger and working to resolve the problems is wasted on demands that individual feelings be a priority above safety.

Politeness as filtered through fragility and supremacy isn't about manners; it's about a methodology of controlling the conversation. Polite white people who respond to calls for respect, for getting boots off necks with demand for decorum, aren't interested in resistance or disruption. They are interested in control. They replicate the manners of Jim Crow America, demanding deference and obedience; they want the polite facade instead of disruption. They insist that they know best what should be done when attempting to battle and defeat bias, but in actuality they're just happy to be useless. They are obstacles to freedom who feel no remorse, who provide no valuable insight, because ultimately, they are content to get in the way. They're oppression tourists, virtue-signaling volunteers who are really just here to get what they can and block the way, so no others can pass without meeting whatever arbitrary standards they create. And if you get enough of them in one place, they can prevent any real progress from occurring while they reap the benefits of straddling white supremacy and being woke. They have less power than they think, than anyone realizes, but like any small predator, they manage to be flashy enough to be seen.

In general, feminism as a career is the province of the privileged; it's hard to read dozens of books on feminist theory while you're working in a hair salon or engaged in the kinds of jobs that put food on the table but also demand a lot of physical and mental energy. For many who are coming to feminism in the way that I did, through lived experience, the work that feminists do in the community is more relevant than any text.

We must understand that any feminist work done in public is supported by the under-recognized, feminized work done by caregivers, sex workers, clerks, and cleaners. We must be careful not to come in as gentrifiers of the feminism that comes out of survival. We have the power to help or to do harm, and the risk imposed on communities by ignoring what has been built—in favor of some idea that we can do it better than the people who have to live with the consequences even when we do not—cannot be ignored.

I'm far from the first person to talk about being an accomplice instead of an ally, and I would certainly never presume to speak for other communities, but I think there are some areas where our concerns overlap. No one needs a savior to ride in, take over, and decide for them what would be the best approach to solve a problem. No one has time to play emotional caretaker for allies who would be accomplices. In general, if you have come to these spaces looking to take things away for your benefit instead of looking to contribute, then you're already doing it wrong.

This is a space where we must be able to have the hard conversations after conflict, because sometimes the political is personal. Being a good accomplice is where the real work gets done. That means taking the risks inherent in wielding privilege to defend communities with less of it, and it means being willing to not just pass the mic but to sometimes get completely off the stage so that someone else can get the attention they need to get their work done. We can't afford to silo the work into what we think counts as a feminist issue and instead must understand that the issues a community faces can cover a wide range, and that being able to eat, see a doctor, work, and sleep in a place free from the dangers of environmental racism are important.

Too often white feminism lies to itself. It lies about intent and impact; it invests more in protecting whiteness than in protecting women. It's not a harmless lie either; it does direct harm to marginalized communities. Being harmful is a source of power that some white feminists have embraced in lieu of actually doing any real work. They get drunk on power and they can't resist the urge to exert it as much as possible. This isn't just about the vicious bigotry that lets Kirstjen Nielsen get on Fox News and blame the death of a seven-year-old girl on her family for the "crime" of seeking asylum. Nor is it just the petty power jolt some white women seem to get from calling the cops. Feminism can't afford to prioritize supporting whiteness over actively combating racist and misogynistic policies that will end up hurting everyone.

The fundamental problem with white feminism has always been that it refuses to admit that the primary goal is shifting power to white women, and no one else. It says that it supports all white women being empowered regardless of whether they are ethical or not. For white feminism, anyone can claim to be an ally as long as they occasionally do the right thing, but the reality is that the performance of allyship is ultimately untrustworthy and useless. It allows white feminism to do damage control with apologies—after incredibly shitty behavior, feminist author Laurie Penny would probably call herself an ally, but she's been absolutely complicit in the validation of white supremacist narratives around culture and race in her work. Though Penny's recognition in "A Letter to my Liberal Friends" that her decision to give Milo Yiannopoulos access to a broader stage is a welcome moment of accountability after the fact, it remains to be seen how much harm can be ameliorated with a few words. She's an ally, all right, but not a good one, and she will probably never be an accomplice because her privilege lets her find people who will accept her performance without expecting any real work from her.

In a way, it makes sense that white feminism reflexively protects white women from consequences of their actions. A movement that wants equal rights to oppress has a vested interest in not cleaning house. But the innately abusive nature of white supremacy has shaped white feminism, seen to it that investment in white supremacy is easier than investment in actual equality for themselves with all women. White feminism has to move past any idea of being an ally and into being an accomplice in order for it to be meaningful.

Accomplice feminists would actively and directly challenge white supremacist people, policies, institutions, and cultural norms. They would know they do not need to have the same stake in the fight to work with marginalized communities. They would put aside their egos and their need to be centered in our struggles in favor of following our instructions, because they would internalize the reality that their privilege doesn't make them experts on our oppression. This style of feminism would be performative, would not pay lip service to equality while sustaining and supporting those who actively work against it. Becoming an accomplice feminist is not simply semantic. Accomplices do not just talk about bigotry; they do something about it.

Accomplice feminists not only address the dangers of the normalization of extreme white supremacist views, they interrogate and challenge the cultural standards that underpin those views. They don't just stand on the sidelines watching while marginalized people are brutalized for protesting, they stand between the white supremacist systems (which are less likely to harm them) and those that the systems are trying to harm. This isn't a single-day fight; this is a commitment to working against white supremacy in the same way that other marginalized communities do.

This goes beyond white feminist savior narratives and into challenging those who are more interested in weaponizing bigotry than in advancing women's rights. We have to get past peak white feminism and into actual feminism. This is not to say that problems within marginalized communities should not be addressed, but they can no longer be used to deflect from the accountability and the work of being an accomplice. Marginalized communities have already developed strategies and solutions as they do their own internal work. Now mainstream feminism has to step up, has to get itself to a place where it spends more time offering resources and less time demanding validation. Being an accomplice means that white feminism will devote its platforms and resources to supporting those in marginalized communities doing feminist work.

ACKNOWLEDGMENTS

For my ancestors, for my community, for my family, and my friends. To the Husbeast, Rugrat, and Karndilla ... thank you. I love you. Thank you to Jill Grinberg, my amazing agent; and Georgia Bodnar, who edited the hell out of this book. This is for Mariah, who wasn't legally allowed to read but made sure her daughters could do what she had not; for Penny Rose, who did what it took; for Dorothy, Denise, Karyce, Penny, and Maria. For Lisa, Pint, Jamie, Chesya, Jackie, Julia, Gatorface, CJ, Justine, Nora, Tempest, Cat, Heather, Sydette, De Ana, Carole, Erin, Beth, Christa, Erika, and so many others who helped me when I needed it. Even when that involved a good swift kick in the pants. To the librarians and the teachers who helped. Chicago: You built me. I hope I did you proud.

SOURCES

GUN VIOLENCE

Statistic on guns in a domestic violence situation, from J. C. Campbell, D. Webster, J. Koziol-McLain, C. Block, D. Campbell, M. A. Curry, F. Gary et al., "Risk Factors for Femicide in Abusive Relationships: Results from a Multisite Case Control Study," *American Journal of Public Health* 93, no. 7 (2003): 1089–97.

Dropout rates of public school students, from R. L. Moore, "The Effects of Exposure to Community Gun-Violence on the High School Dropout Rates of California Public School Students" (PhD diss., University of California, Los Angeles, 2018), https://escholarship.org/uc/item/4gf4v5c7.

Statistics on gun-related deaths of American children, from "The Impact of Gun Violence on Children and Teens," Everytown, May 29, 2019, https://everytownresearch.org/impact-gun-violence-american-children-teens/.

Marty Langley and Josh Sugarmann quote from Violence Policy Center, appears in *Black Homicide Victimization in the United States: An Analysis of 2015 Homicide Data* (Washington, DC: Violence Policy Center, 2018), http://vpc.org/studies/blackhomicide18.pdf.

HUNGER

Studies by the Centers for Disease Control and Prevention can be found in Emily Dollar, Margit Berman, and Anna M. Adachi-Mejia, "Do No

Harm: Moving Beyond Weight Loss to Emphasize Physical Activity at Every Size," *Preventing Chronic Disease* 14 (2017), https://www.cdc.gov/pcd/issues/2017/17_0006.htm.

OF #FASTTAILEDGIRLS AND FREEDOM

Emily Yoffe, "College Women: Stop Getting Drunk," *Slate*, October 15, 2013, https://slate.com/human-interest/2013/10/sexual-assault-and-drinking-teach-women-the-connection.html.

Amanda Marcotte, "Prosecutors Arrest Alleged Rape Victim to Make Her Cooperate in Their Case. They Made the Right Call," *Slate*, February 25, 2014, https://slate.com/human-interest/2014/02/alleged-rape-victim-arrested-to-force-her-to-cooperate-in-the-case-against-her-abusers.html.

On white bystanders helping, from J. W. Kunstman and E. A. Plant, "Racing to Help: Racial Bias in High Emergency Helping Situations," *Journal of Personality and Social Psychology* 95, no. 6 (2008): 1499–510, https://www.ncbi.nlm.nih.gov/pubmed/19025298.

White women bystanders, from Jennifer Katz, Christine Merrilees, Jill C. Hoxmeier, and Marisa Motisi, "White Female Bystanders' Responses to a Black Woman at Risk for Incapacitated Sexual Assault," *Psychology of Women Quarterly* 41, no. 2 (2017): 273–85, https://journals.sagepub.com/doi/10.1177/0361684316689367.

Lena Dunham's apology, from "Lena Dunham: My Apology to Aurora," *Hollywood Reporter*, December 5, 2018, https://www.hollywoodreporter.com/news/lena-dunham-my-apology-aurora-perrineau-1165614.

IT'S RAINING PATRIARCHY

Homicide rates research, from Natalia E. Pane, "Data Point: Gun Violence Is the Most Common Cause of Death for Young Men," Child Trends, February 22, 2018, https://www.childtrends.org/gun-violence-common-cause-death-young-men.

The study from Georgetown Law's Center on Poverty and Inequality, from Rebecca Epstein, Jamilia J. Blake, and Thalia González, *Girlhood Interrupted: The Erasure of Black Girls' Childhood* (Washington, DC: Georgetown Law's Center on Poverty and Inequality, 2017), https://www.law.georgetown.edu/poverty-inequality-center/wp-content/uploads/sites/14/2017/08/girlhood-interrupted.pdf.

Dehumanizing Black children, from Phillip Atiba Goff, Matthew Christian Jackson, Brooke Allison, Lewis Di Leone, Carmen Marie Culotta, and Natalie Ann DiTomasso, "The Essence of Innocence: Consequences of Dehumanizing Black Children," *Journal of Personality and Social Psychology* 106, no. 4 (2014): 526–45, https://www.apa.org/pubs/journals/releases /psp-a0035663.pdf.

Collier Meyerson, "A Hollaback Response Video: Women of Color on Street Harassment," *Jezebel* (blog), November 6, 2014, https://jezebel.com/a -hollaback-response-video-women-of-color-on-street-ha-1655494647.

PRETTY FOR A . . .

Discrimination against people with locs, from Lee Peifer, "Eleventh Circuit Declines to Revisit Dreadlocks Discrimination Case en Banc," *11thCircuitBusinessBlog.com*, December 18, 2017, https://www.11thcircuitbusinessblog.com /2017/12/eleventh-circuit-declines-to-revisit-dreadlocks-discrimination -case-en-banc/.

BLACK GIRLS DON'T HAVE EATING DISORDERS

On health-care providers, from Angela Garbes, "America Is Utterly Failing People of Color with Eating Disorders," *Splinter*, May 7, 2017, https:// splinternews.com/how-america-fails-people-of-color-with-eating -disorders-1793858224.

Being overweight doesn't increase mortality, from K. M. Flegal, B. I. Graubard, D. F. Williamson, and M. H. Gail, "Excess Deaths Associated with Underweight, Overweight, and Obesity," *JAMA* 293, no. 15 (2005): 1861–7, https://www.ncbi.nlm.nih.gov/pubmed/15840860.

The assumption that eating disorders largely affect white women, from K. H. Gordon, M. Perez, and T. E. Joiner Jr., "The Impact of Racial Stereotypes on Eating Disorder Recognition," *International Journal of Eating Disorders* 32, no. 2 (2002): 219–24, https://www.ncbi.nlm.nih.gov/pubmed /12210665/.

Cultural competence in the treatment of eating disorders, from Debra L. Franko, "Race, Ethnicity, and Eating Disorders: Considerations for DSM-V," *International Journal of Eating Disorders* 40 (2007): S31–4, https:// onlinelibrary.wiley.com/doi/pdf/10.1002/eat.20455.

MISSING AND MURDERED

Murder rates in Chicago, from Aamer Madhani, "Unsolved Murders: Chicago, Other Big Cities Struggle; Murder Rate a 'National Disaster,'" *USA Today*, August 10, 2018, https://www.usatoday.com/story/news/2018/08/10/u-s-homicide-clearance-rate-crisis/951681002/.

A serial killer in Chicago, from Kelly Bauer, "Is There a Serial Killer Targeting Black Women in Chicago? After 50 Women Slain, FBI and CPD Form Task Force to Investigate," Block Club Chicago, April 12, 2019, https://blockclub chicago.org/2019/04/12/police-fbi-task-force-investigating-if-slayings -of-50-women-mostly-black-are-work-of-serial-killer/.

Missing Indigenous women, from Camila Domonoske, "Police in Many U.S. Cities Fail to Track Murdered, Missing Indigenous Women," NPR, November 15, 2018, https://www.npr.org/2018/11/15/667335392/police-in -many-u-s-cities-fail-to-track-murdered-missing-indigenous-women.

The study from the Urban Indian Health Institute can be found at Annita Lucchesi and Abigail Echo-Hawk, *Missing and Murdered Indigenous Women and Girls: A Snapshot of Data from 71 Urban Cities in the United States* (Seattle: Urban Indian Health Institute, 2019), http://www.uihi .org/wp-content/uploads/2018/11/Missing-and-Murdered-Indigenous -Women-and-Girls-Report.pdf.

The homicide rate of Indigenous women, from David K. Espey, Melissa A. Jim, Nathaniel Cobb, Michael Bartholomew, Tom Becker, Don Haverkamp, and Marcus Plescia, "Leading Causes of Death and All-Cause Mortality in American Indians and Alaska Natives," *American Journal of Public Health* 104, suppl. 3 (2014): S303–11, https://www.ncbi.nlm.nih.gov/pmc/articles /PMC4035872/.

Women from Central America seeking asylum, from Chiara Cardoletti-Carroll, Alice Farmer, and Leslie E. Vélez, eds., *Women on the Run* (Washington, DC: United Nations High Commissioner for Refugees, 2015), https://www.unhcr.org/5630f24c6.html.

Rates of violence against trans people in the US, from a report from Mark Lee, *A National Epidemic: Fatal Anti-Transgender Violence in America in 2018* (Washington, DC: Human Rights Campaign, 2018), https://www .hrc.org/resources/a-national-epidemic-fatal-anti-transgender-violence -in-america-in-2018.

RACE, POVERTY, AND POLITICS

Bill Clinton on not inhaling, from Olivia B. Waxman, "Bill Clinton Said He 'Didn't Inhale' 25 Years Ago—But the History of U.S. Presidents and Drugs Is Much Older," *Time*, March 29, 2017, http://time.com/4711887 /bill-clinton-didnt-inhale-marijuana-anniversary/.

Quote from Diana Mutz, from Tom Jacobs, "Research Finds That Racism, Sexism, and Status Fears Drove Trump Voters," *Pacific Standard*, April 24, 2018, https://psmag.com/news/research-finds-that-racism-sexism-and-status -fears-drove-trump-voters.

More on Bernie Bros from Dara Lind, "Bernie Bros, Explained," *Vox*, February 5, 2016, https://www.vox.com/2016/2/4/10918710/berniebro-bernie-bro.

Sentencing Project's May 2018 report can be found at "Incarcerated Women and Girls," Sentencing Project, June 6, 2019, https://www.sentencingpro ject.org/publications/incarcerated-women-and-girls/.

EDUCATION

Study of students in an alternative school setting, from Kathryn S. Whitted and David R. Dupper, "Do Teachers Bully Students? Findings from a Survey of Students in an Alternative Education Setting," *Education and Urban Society* 40, no. 3 (2007): 329–41, https://journals.sagepub.com /doi/abs/10.1177/0013124507304487.

On $5.7 billion a year being spent on the juvenile justice system, from Amanda Petteruti, Marc Schindler, and Jason Ziedenberg, *Sticker Shock: Calculating the Full Price Tag for Youth Incarceration* (Washington, DC: Justice Policy Institute, 2014), http://www.justicepolicy.org/uploads/ justicepolicy/documents/sticker_shock_final_v2.pdf.

Chicago's school closures, from Linda Lutton, Becky Vevea, Sarah Karp, Adriana Cardona-Maguidad, and Kate McGee, "A Generation of School Closings," WBEZ, December 3, 2018, https://interactive.wbez.org/generation -school-closings/.

Data on the disciplining of Black students, from a fact sheet published by the National Education Policy Center, Annenberg Institute for School Reform, and Dignity in Schools Campaign, "School Discipline Myths and Facts," Dignity in Schools, https://dignityinschools.org/resources/school -discipline-myths-and-facts-3/.

Data on the arrests of Black students, from Evie Blad and Corey Mitchell, "Black Students Bear Uneven Brunt of Discipline, Data Show," *Education Week*, May 1, 2018, https://www.edweek.org/ew/articles/2018/05/02/black -students-bear-uneven-brunt-of-discipline.html.

HOUSING

Eviction cases in 2016 and Matthew Desmond's Eviction Lab, from Terry Gross, "First-Ever Evictions Database Shows: 'We're in the Middle of a Housing Crisis,'" NPR, April 12, 2018, https://www.npr.org/2018/04/12 /601783346/first-ever-evictions-database-shows-were-in-the-middle -of-a-housing-crisis.

REPRODUCTIVE JUSTICE, EUGENICS, AND MATERNAL MORTALITY

Maternal mortality rates, from Nina Martin, ProPublica, Renee Montagne, and NPR News, "Nothing Protects Black Women from Dying in Pregnancy and Childbirth," ProPublica, December 7, 2017, https://www.propublica .org/article/nothing-protects-black-women-from-dying-in-pregnancy -and-childbirth.

Forced sterilization of Indigenous women, from Erin Blakemore, "The Little-Known History of the Forced Sterilization of Native American Women," *JSTOR Daily*, August 25, 2016, https://daily.jstor.org/the-little-known -history-of-the-forced-sterilization-of-native-american-women/.

Forced sterilization of Latina women, from Katherine Andrews, "The Dark History of Forced Sterilization of Latina Women," Panoramas, October 30, 2017, https://www.panoramas.pitt.edu/health-and-society/dark-history -forced-sterilization-latina-women.

Forced sterilization of inmates, from Reuters, "California Bans Sterilization of Female Inmates Without Consent," *NBC News*, September 26, 2014, https:// www.nbcnews.com/health/womens-health/california-bans-sterilization -female-inmates-without-consent-n212256.

On aborting fetuses with disabilities, from Lawrence B. Finer, Lori F. Frohwirth, Lindsay A. Dauphinee, Susheela Singh, and Ann M. Moore, "Reasons U.S. Women Have Abortions: Quantitative and Qualitative Perspectives," *Perspectives on Sexual and Reproductive Health* 37, no. 3

(2005): 110–18, https://www.guttmacher.org/journals/psrh/2005/reasons-us-women-have-abortions-quantitative-and-qualitative-perspectives.

Forced sterilization of people with disabilities, from S. E. Smith, "Disabled People Are Still Being Forcibly Sterilized—So Why Isn't Anyone Talking About It?" *Rewire.News*, November 17, 2014, https://rewire.news/article/2014/11/17/disabled-people-still-forcibly-sterilized-isnt-anyone-talking/.

Racism on social media, from Vic Micolucci, "Baby Posts at Jacksonville Hospital Prompt Global Response from Navy," *News4Jax*, September 20, 2017, https://www.news4jax.com/news/baby-posts-at-jacksonville-hospital-prompt-global-response-from-navy.

On Beyoncé Knowles-Carter's pregnancy, from Derecka Purnell, "If Even Beyoncé Had a Rough Pregnancy, What Hope Do Other Black Women Have?" *Guardian*, April 23, 2019, https://www.theguardian.com/commentisfree/2019/apr/23/beyonce-pregnancy-black-women.

ALLIES, ANGER, AND ACCOMPLICES

Laurie Penny, "A Letter to my Liberal Friends," *The Baffler*, August 15, 2017, https://thebaffler.com/war-of-nerves/a-letter-to-my-liberal-friends.